95

THE INN OF DISCONTENT

AND

OTHER FANTASTIC PLAYS

THE INN OF DISCONTENT
AND
OTHER FANTASTIC PLAYS

BY

PERCIVAL WILDE

BOSTON
LITTLE, BROWN, AND COMPANY
1924

PREFACE

Iᴛ is with a certain trepidation that the author offers this, his fifth volume of collected plays. In the interval which has elapsed since the appearance of his fourth volume, he has had the temerity to put forward a work on the subject of technique, "The Craftsmanship of the One-Act Play", and in view of that circumstance, he is only too well aware that his own plays, now and in the future, will be judged by increasingly severe standards.

With that condition, he has no fault to find. If he, however modestly, has contributed to the elevation of those standards, he is content, whatever the result to himself. The perfection of any art matters more than the fate of any practitioner of it; the ultimate destiny of a drop of water is less significant than the fact that it has added itself to the ocean.

Some of the plays in this volume have taken long periods of time to arrive at maturity; one, indeed, has spread its adolescent existence over more than five years, and has passed through more than a dozen drafts in the process of finding itself. Yet the author, reading over his pages, is but too painfully conscious that but one Author, since the beginning of time, could look upon his work and in all confidence say that it was good.

Certain definite thoughts have gone to the making of these plays. No man — and surely no woman — is so simple a character that a mere thumbnail sketch may epitomize him. These plays body forth certain facts about their characters: but there is not one of those characters, the author likes to believe, about whom more interesting plays might not well be conceived. The character, in a word, is superior to the play: existed before it did; will continue to exist after it is ended. The play is merely one of many that might be written about him: it surveys the ground; it cannot preëmpt more than a small part of it.

Yet since the picture cannot hope to show all, it must strive to suggest, to summon up in the minds of the beholders thoughts so inarticulate, perhaps, that they may not be phrased in words. The play is on the stage, but a better play, a profounder play, a more searching play, must parallel it in the imaginings of its audience. This conception, too, has been fundamental in these pages, for while it is the visible that crowds upon us in our everyday life, it is the invisible, the spiritual, the quest after the forever unattainable that leads us upwards in our struggles.

SHARON, CONNECTICUT.
  July, 1924.

CONTENTS

THE INN OF DISCONTENT

A FANTASTIC PLAY
IN THREE SCENES

CHARACTERS

An Old Man
A Lover
A Scientist
A Poet
A Serious Individual
A Girl
A Young Thing
An Old Woman

THE INN OF DISCONTENT

THE FIRST SCENE

Outside

Night. A great portal. Over it, a hanging lantern. On either side of it, lofty windows. A path winds from right to left. The scene is but dimly lighted.

THE POET

I wonder if the door will ever open.

THE SCIENTIST

The door is opening.

THE POET

About time, I should say.

[Slowly the door swings inward just far enough to permit an old man to stand upon the threshold.

His appearance is curious. His clothes are rather less than informal. His trousers are old and baggy at the knees; he wears neither coat, collar, tie, nor hat; and his unbuttoned vest flaps over an untidy shirt. His glistening bald scalp, fringed by a few lonely hairs on either side, surmounts an easy-going, humor-loving, contented countenance. The total impression he conveys is that of a sixty-year-old bricklayer at a moment of relaxation.

THE POET (*sotto voce to the Scientist*)

They don't put on much style here, do they? Nothing pretentious — nothing impressive — nothing palatial. Judging by the gatekeeper it is n't much of an Inn.

THE OLD MAN (*overhearing; placidly*)

It ain't.

THE POET

Oh, I beg your pardon. I did n't mean to offend you.

THE OLD MAN

I ain't offended. Who said I was? I don't take offense easy. No, sir! Not me! When you 've seen as much as I have, an' when you 've lived as long as me, you learn to take 'em as they come without getting het up about it. Easy 's the word — easy. (*He seats himself comfortably on the threshold. It is to be noted that at no time does he actually cross it*) No; it ain't much of an Inn — I 'll say so — but it 's the only one there is. Leastways, it 's the only one I know about. So you can take it, or you can leave it.

THE POET

Why did n't you come when we knocked?

THE OLD MAN

Did you knock?

THE SCIENTIST

We knocked twice.

THE OLD MAN

In the first place, I ain't the gatekeeper. There ain't no gatekeeper here. But leaving that aside, why did you knock at all? What 's the big idea? Why did n't you walk right in?

THE POET

What?

THE OLD MAN

The door 's never locked. It 's always open. You can come in, or you can get out, just as suits you best. Only once you go, you can't come back.

See? (*He extracts a stubby clay pipe from a pocket, and lights it contentedly*) Got to make up your mind — that's all there's to it. Got to decide what you want to do — and then stick to it. (*He pauses*) Some stays; some don't. Some thinks it's great; some thinks it's rotten. Some likes it; some hates it. Now, I likes it. I thinks —

THE POET (*interrupting*)

Can you put us up overnight?

THE OLD MAN

We're full.

THE POET

You can't turn us away on a night like this.

THE OLD MAN

What's the matter with the night? Like any other night, ain't it?

THE POET

You can't turn us away; that's all.

THE OLD MAN

I ain't said nothing about turning you away. Not a word! (*He appeals to the Scientist*) Ain't that so, mister?

THE SCIENTIST

You can put us up somewheres.

THE OLD MAN

"Put us up?" "Put us up?" How do you get that way? You can go in if you like. You can find a room if you like.

THE SCIENTIST

But you said you were full.

THE OLD MAN

Sure. We're always full. There's never been a day

since I've been here that we ain't been full. But what's that got to do with it? We won't be no fuller to-morrow than we are to-day — and we won't be no fuller next week than we'll be to-morrow. Go on in. Find a room. Find a good room while you're at it. If there's somebody in it, put him out.

THE POET (*surprised*)

What? What did you say?

THE OLD MAN

Put him out, I said. Put him out. O-u-t; out.

THE SCIENTIST

Put him out where?

THE OLD MAN (*genially*)

Well, that's what you might call a matter of taste. Throw him downstairs. Pitch him out of the window if that strikes your fancy. Do what you like, only get rid of him somehow.

THE POET (*hesitantly*)

I have no inclination for that sort of thing. I'm quite sure I'd prefer not to do that.

THE OLD MAN

You don't have to.

THE POET

If I find a room I like, I might ask the man in it to double up with me.

THE OLD MAN

You might.

THE POET

He might be willing to do that.

THE OLD MAN

He might.

THE POET

Then again —

THE SCIENTIST

He might *not* be willing. He might throw *you* downstairs. He might pitch *you* out of the window.

THE OLD MAN (*nodding*)

You 're beginning to get the idea.

THE POET

Look here — what about the law?

THE OLD MAN

Well, what about it?

THE POET

There should be something of the kind —

THE OLD MAN (*interrupting*)

Laws! Laws! Do you want some laws? All right, go ahead and make some. Go right ahead. Make some every morning when you get up. Make some after breakfast. Make some more after lunch. Make some more every night.

THE POET

But have n't you got any already?

THE OLD MAN

They give me a headache. That 's what I think of 'em.

THE POET (*shaking his head*)

I don't want to put anybody out. Rather than do that, I 'd sleep on the floor.

THE OLD MAN

You can. You can. Some try that a while.

THE SCIENTIST

What happens?

THE OLD MAN

They get tired of it.   But there's nothing to prevent
you from trying it if you like.   In fact, you can try
anything you like.

THE SCIENTIST (*after a pause*)

I think we should do as the others do.

THE OLD MAN

If you're asking me, that seems to be the general
sentiment.

THE SCIENTIST (*resolutely*)

Come on; I'm going in.

THE POET (*hesitantly*)

I'd rather not.

THE OLD MAN

Suit yourself.   You don't have to come in.   Nevertheless —

THE POET (*as he pauses*)

Nevertheless?

THE OLD MAN (*kindly*)

I've noticed — they get used to it pretty fast.

THE SCIENTIST

Come.   I'm going in.

THE POET

So am I.

[*They enter the Inn.*

The old man smiles; puffs his pipe.

*Presently a Young Thing enters from one side.   She
is buoyant, pretty, and, according to her own con-
ceptions of how such details should be managed, is
dressed to kill.*

THE YOUNG THING

Hello, old bean!

THE OLD MAN

Hello, yourself!

THE YOUNG THING

Pretty quiet, eh?

THE OLD MAN

Always quiet, to my way of thinking.

THE YOUNG THING

Is that so? Well, wait till I get inside, and I'll show 'em something. I'll put some pep in the old joint. I'll make 'em sit up all right, all right!

THE OLD MAN

There's always use for somebody like you.

THE YOUNG THING

Ain't it the truth? A little bunch of perpetual motion — that's me! A hundred and ten pounds of chain lightning — all in one package! I'm out for a good time — a r'aring, tearing good time — and I don't care who knows it. The more, the better. (*She stops; peers at the doorway with odd, birdlike motions of her head*) You know, if I was running things, I'd change all this.

THE OLD MAN

How so?

THE YOUNG THING

I'd make it more friendly. It isn't friendly enough — not for me, at any rate. I'd put a couple of nice, comfortable seats here — one on either side of the door; and I'd plant rambler roses all around; and I'd hang gay curtains in the windows. And then I'd lay a mat down — there's something friendly about a mat — and I'd put up a sign "Welcome Stranger." I'd make it a bit homey, see? (*Hesitantly; wistfully*) Do you think they'd allow it?

THE OLD MAN

I'm afraid it can't be done.

THE YOUNG THING

No, I guess not. You can never do anything you really want to, can you? (*She pauses*) Say, is it like this on the inside?

THE OLD MAN

What do you mean?

THE YOUNG THING

Dark — cold — unfriendly — ?

THE OLD MAN

I'm not unfriendly.

THE YOUNG THING

No, but the rest — the rest of everything?

THE OLD MAN

Inside — inside — it's what you make it.

THE YOUNG THING (*eagerly*)

Do you mean that?

THE OLD MAN

What you make it? Yes, I mean that; every word.

THE YOUNG THING (*with relief*)

Then it won't be so bad after all. (*She inspects the doorway again*) Come to think of it, it doesn't look so unfriendly when you get used to it. I think — I think I could get to like it —

THE OLD MAN

Bully for you.

THE YOUNG THING (*finishing her sentence*)

— if the inside's nicer. (*She pauses; pirouettes gaily on the threshold*) What a lark it's going to be! What a lark! Things will be different now that I'm here!
[*She pirouettes into the Inn.*

THE OLD MAN (*calling after her*)

Good luck to you!

[*A pause. It is slowly growing lighter.*
Presently a Lover and a Girl come along the path.

THE LOVER

Just a few steps more, sweetheart.

THE GIRL

You've been saying that all night.

THE LOVER

But it's only a short distance now.

THE GIRL

I'm tired; I'm so tired.

THE LOVER

Don't you see? We're there, dearest.

THE GIRL

It's been such a long way; such a terribly long way.

THE LOVER

We've come to the end of it.

THE GIRL

The beginning of it; only the beginning of it. I feel as if I couldn't take another step.

THE LOVER

Dearest, we're nearly at the threshold. It's only a little further.

THE GIRL

I must rest first. (*She sits*) I'm so tired; so tired.

THE LOVER

Rest; rest as long as you like, and then, when you're ready, we'll go in. Haven't we been looking forward to that, it seems for ages and ages?

THE GIRL

Don't ask me. I'm tired. I can't think. I want to rest; that's all.

THE OLD MAN

Good evening, sir — and ma'am.

THE LOVER

Good evening.

THE OLD MAN

A fine night. A remarkably fine night, if I say so myself.

THE LOVER

A fine night, indeed.

THE OLD MAN (*offering his pouch*)

A bit of 'baccy?

THE LOVER

Thank you, no. (*He surveys the portal*) So this is the Inn?

THE OLD MAN

Such as it is; yes, sir.

THE LOVER

It's not what you might call prepossessing, at least, not from the outside. I can't say I care for it.

THE OLD MAN (*nodding*)

There's many of 'em that don't.

THE LOVER (*peering across the threshold*)

Uninviting; gloomy; a dark, depressing place: that's how it strikes me.

THE OLD MAN

Some find it so.

THE LOVER

But it's the only one there is, therefore it's the best

there is. That's logical. It's the best of all possible
Inns.

THE OLD MAN

That's one of my own ways of looking at it, sir.

THE LOVER

After all, it's not the place that matters. It's what
you bring to it. It's not what's around you : it's
what you've got inside of yourself.

THE OLD MAN

Ah, there you've said a true word !

THE LOVER

I come expecting — well, I hardly know what I
expect. I only know that it will all be new and
strange. But there are two faces to everything,
and I shall look for the pleasanter face. Happiness?
Unhappiness? What are they? Castles you build
out of nothing. Where are they? Within yourself!
Your world is what you think it is — you, and you
alone. Mine shall be a glorious world, filled with
lovely things, overflowing with beautiful moments, a
long succession of happy hours !

THE OLD MAN

A great idea, sir, if you can hold on to it.

THE LOVER

Of course I shall hold on to it. What makes you
think anything else might happen? I shall hold on
to it : nothing simpler.

THE OLD MAN

It ain't always the simplest things that are the easiest.

THE LOVER

Humph ! (*He returns to the Girl*) Are you rested,
sweetheart ?

THE GIRL

Yes, dear.

THE LOVER

Are you ready to go in?

THE GIRL

In a little while. (*She rises; goes to him*) Dear, you love me?

THE LOVER

I love you.

THE GIRL

Much?

THE LOVER

Very much. More than anything else.

THE GIRL

Are you sure? Are you quite sure?

THE LOVER

It is the one thing of which I am sure.

THE GIRL

It is the one thing of which we must be sure. On that we are resting all our faith. If we should be mistaken — if we should be deceiving ourselves, it would be too terrible.

THE LOVER (*resolutely*)

We are not deceiving ourselves.

THE GIRL

We met — as in a dream. Two souls — two human souls — wandering in a mist. We met. We loved. We love.

THE LOVER

We will always love.

THE GIRL

Ah, if I only knew!

THE LOVER (*taking her in his arms*)

Everything else may be unreal. For all we know, everything else is unreal. But our love, that is not unreal! Wherever you go — wherever I go — our love will draw us together.

THE GIRL

Do you believe that? Do you really believe that?

THE LOVER

With all my heart. From the ends of the earth my love will call to you —

THE GIRL

And from the ends of the earth my love will answer. [*They kiss.*

THE OLD MAN

Ahem! Ahem!

THE LOVER

What is it?

THE OLD MAN

There might be others coming any moment.

THE LOVER

We don't care. Do we? Let them see. What is there to be ashamed of? (*He leads the Girl towards the Old Man*) This lady has promised to become my wife.

THE GIRL

We met — it seems ages ago.

THE OLD MAN (*without addressing anybody in particular*)

It 'most always does.

THE GIRL

We loved at sight. We will always love.

THE OLD MAN

I seem to have heard those words before.

THE GIRL

Whatever happens, whatever may come, our love will draw us together.

THE OLD MAN

Even in there?

THE GIRL

Even in there.

THE OLD MAN

Fine if it works. Fine and dandy!

THE LOVER (*bristling*)

Are you suggesting it won't work?

THE OLD MAN

I ain't suggesting anything. I'm just saying —

THE LOVER (*interrupting*)

You're saying too much. (*He turns to the Girl*) Come, dearest.

[*They enter the Inn together.*

THE OLD MAN

So that's that!

[*He proceeds philosophically to knock the ashes out of his pipe.*

Down the path comes a Serious Individual. It is now sunrise.

THE OLD MAN

Good evening.

THE SERIOUS INDIVIDUAL

Good evening — I should say, good morning.

THE OLD MAN

Anything you like. Good morning it is.

THE SERIOUS INDIVIDUAL

The Inn is open?

THE OLD MAN

The Inn is always open.

THE SERIOUS INDIVIDUAL

I shall go in.

THE OLD MAN

That is your privilege.

THE SERIOUS INDIVIDUAL

I have heard a great deal about the Inn. I want to know more about it. I want to find out all there is to find out about it.

THE OLD MAN

Ah?

THE SERIOUS INDIVIDUAL

I have heard that the Inn is run very badly. I have ideas of my own on the subject. I shall see that the Inn is run according to my ideas.

THE OLD MAN

Others have tried.

THE SERIOUS INDIVIDUAL

I shall succeed. Good morning.

[*He enters the Inn.*

THE CURTAIN FALLS

THE SECOND SCENE

Inside

Morning. The inner side of the portal, open. On either side of it, lofty windows. Through portal and windows one sees a background which is brilliantly illuminated, but which is quite featureless — skyey — neither earth nor trees nor clouds. Only a chair or two serves to show that we are indoors.

At one window, peering out intently, is the Scientist.

Offstage voices:

THE POET

What are they all doing?

THE OLD MAN

Trying to find happiness.

THE POET

And how are they doing that?

THE OLD MAN

By running away from it — by running away from it just as hard as they can.

THE POET

Do they ever find happiness?

THE OLD MAN

Sometimes — when it catches up with them.

[*He enters at the right.*

THE SCIENTIST

Oh, it's you? I've been waiting for you. Come here. Look.

THE OLD MAN

Look at what?

THE SCIENTIST

Through the windows.   What do you see?

THE OLD MAN (*with patient indulgence*)

What do you want me to see?

THE SCIENTIST

Nothing.

THE OLD MAN

Very well, then; I see nothing.

THE SCIENTIST

That's what I claim.   Once you cross the threshold there is nothing — nothing at all.   Emptiness — blank — Nirvana — oblivion — the candle snuffed out and extinguished.   It's scientifically demonstrable.   What is there beyond?   Distance?   Immensity?   Infinity?   Boundless   space?   Other   Inns like this one?   I doubt it.

THE OLD MAN (*nodding sagely*)

You doubt it.

THE SCIENTIST

The threshold is the boundary line.   Here everything begins — here everything ends.   The boundary line — the jumping-off place — the barrier between the something and the not-something.   On one side, life, warmth, light, joy, sadness, fear, envy, struggle, hope, aspiration, triumph, victory, defeat.   On the other side, as you said so eloquently, nothing.

THE OLD MAN

Great flow of language — I gotta hand it to you. But what gets me —

[*He pauses.*

THE SCIENTIST (*kindly*)

Go on.   Don't be afraid.   I'll answer your questions.

THE OLD MAN

What gets me is this : how do you know on which side
you are now?

THE SCIENTIST

Eh? What's that?

THE OLD MAN

I was only asking how you knew on which side you
was now.

THE SCIENTIST

Don't *you* know?

THE OLD MAN

I ain't sure. I ain't sure at all. You see, when I
was a young fellow, there was n't much I was n't sure
about; but it's changed as I've grown older. As I
get along in years the two sides begin to look a lot
alike; an' sometimes I wonder if there ain't p'rhaps
more than two sides — if there ain't a dozen
sides.

THE POET (*entering from the right, watch in hand*)

I beg your pardon.

THE OLD MAN

Yes, sonny?

THE POET

It's curious, but my watch seems to have stopped.
Have you any idea of the time?

THE OLD MAN

Tst! Tst! Stopped so early! We can fix that in
half a second. What time would you like it to
be?

THE POET (*smiling*)

Well, if it's as simple as that, I think I should like it
to be morning.

THE OLD MAN

Very well, then, morning it is — morning for you —
nine o'clock, if you like.

THE POET (*setting his watch*)

Thank you.

[*He goes.*

THE OLD MAN (*calling after him*)

's all right. Don't mention it. You're entirely welcome. (*He turns to the Scientist*) Morning for him.
For us — what?

THE SCIENTIST

Sh! Sh! (*Feebly, but with great dignity, an Old
Lady has entered at one side. Slowly, painfully, she
moves toward the great door*)
Watch! Now watch!
(*The Old Lady reaches the threshold, casts a last
lingering look about the room she is leaving, smiles, and
goes out. Perhaps she goes to one side; perhaps she goes
straight out. But one does not see her pass the windows*)
Watch! (*A pause*) What did you see?

THE OLD MAN (*who has not looked*)

Nothing.

THE SCIENTIST (*triumphantly*)

Nothing! Nothing at all, exactly as I said. Now
some people will tell you that where there's an inside,
there must be an outside: that there can't be one
without the other. But I say that doesn't follow.
I say nothing follows unless I want it to follow.
Give me proof, and I'll believe. I'm open to conviction: I'm always open to conviction. But I have
yet to find anything quite so reliable as my own
intelligence. I can depend upon that.

THE OLD MAN

Because it tells you what you want to hear?

THE SCIENTIST

Because it is trained to reject myth — superstition — falsehood — call it what you will. Because it cuts away everything from the heart of the subject.

THE OLD MAN

P'rhaps it cuts that away too.

THE SCIENTIST

Humph! Not likely!

[*He turns back to the window.*
There enters the Girl of the first scene.

THE OLD MAN

Good morning, miss.

THE GIRL

Good morning.   It's a lovely morning, isn't it?

THE OLD MAN

Lovely if you say so, miss.

THE GIRL

And if I don't?

THE OLD MAN

Then it ain't.   It's morning — morning for you — and it's just as lovely as you think it is.

THE GIRL

But no lovelier?

THE OLD MAN

Nary a bit.

THE GIRL (*laughing*)

That makes it pleasant.

THE OLD MAN

I'm glad to hear that. I'm glad when anything is pleasant for anybody.

4

THE GIRL (*surveying him curiously*)

It seems to me that I have seen you before.

THE OLD MAN

Yes, miss?

THE GIRL

There's something very familiar about your face. Haven't we met?

THE OLD MAN

I shouldn't be surprised.

THE GIRL

Where was it? (*She pauses*) And when was it? Was it ten years ago? Was it an eternity ago? Was it — last night?

THE OLD MAN

Perhaps it was all three.

THE GIRL (*slowly*)

Perhaps it was.

THE OLD MAN

If it happened — it happened. That's enough, ain't it?

THE GIRL

I seem to recall speaking to you. It becomes clearer in my mind as I think of it. I seem to recall telling you something —

THE OLD MAN

Yes, miss?

THE GIRL

Though for the life of me I can't remember what I told you.

THE OLD MAN

No? Then it can't have been very important.

THE GIRL (*thoughtfully*)

Perhaps it was n't. Perhaps it was n't. And yet — it seems to me that it was very important to me at the time. It seems to me that when I spoke of it, it was more important than anything else in the world —

THE OLD MAN

In the world?

THE GIRL

Or out of it.

THE OLD MAN

Or out of it.

(*They look at each other silently. There is a pause. From the right there enters the Lover of the first scene, crossing the room jauntily. The Girl sees him — starts a little, as with a dim memory. He looks at her with absolute lack of recognition.*

Her start may be interpreted as a bow. He lifts his hat formally, proceeds across the stage, and off at the left.

The Old Man has watched her intently. Her gaze meets his)

Well?

THE GIRL

Well? Did it have something to do with him? — what I am trying to remember? It 's like a dream — a dream that I 've almost forgotten. Was *he* in it? (*As the Old Man does not answer*) Oh, help me! Help me!

THE OLD MAN (*gently*)

How can I help you?

THE GIRL

Help me to look into my heart. Help me to find the

answer. It's on the very tip of my tongue. But I'm groping in the dark. I can't find it myself.

THE OLD MAN

You've got to find it yourself. That's the way things are done here.

THE GIRL

But *you* know — and a word from you —

THE OLD MAN

Would spoil everything. (*He pauses*) What you can't find for yourself isn't worth finding.

THE YOUNG THING (*entering tumultuously*)

Hello, everybody! How's tricks? Say, did you see my fellow around here? Strictly speaking, he isn't my fellow, because we haven't met yet — see? But what's that between friends? The moment I set my lamps on him, I picked him out for yours truly, and that's the same thing.

THE OLD MAN

What's he look like?

THE YOUNG THING

Don't you know him? He's a nice-looking boy, and he dresses something swell.

THE OLD MAN

I think he went that way.

THE YOUNG THING

Then that's the way for me. Much obliged.
[*She starts to go.*

THE GIRL

Wait a minute. How do you know he's your "fellow"?

THE YOUNG THING (*aggressively*)

I seen him first, didn't I? Finding's keepings.

[*She goes, left.*

THE OLD MAN (*to the Girl*)

Well?

THE GIRL

Well?

THE OLD MAN (*to the Scientist*)

What do you think about it?

THE SCIENTIST

I don't.

THE OLD MAN

What do you mean?

THE SCIENTIST

I'm not in the least interested. To me, it's highly unimportant.

[*He goes, right.*

THE SERIOUS INDIVIDUAL (*who has been standing at the right for the last minute*)

I say it's not unimportant. (*He turns and calls after the Scientist*) I say it's anything but unimportant. I say it's very important — very important indeed. (*He goes to the Girl*) I take it for granted that you don't approve.

THE GIRL

Why not?

THE SERIOUS INDIVIDUAL

She openly admitted that they hadn't been introduced to each other. You heard that, didn't you?

THE GIRL

Yes.

THE SERIOUS INDIVIDUAL

Well, that's all wrong. It won't do at all. I shall
make a law providing for just such cases. For the
first infraction (*he rubs his hands with a happy smile*)
there will be a penalty of fine *or* imprisonment;
for the second infraction, fine *and* imprisonment;
for the third — if there should be a third —

THE OLD MAN

Boil 'em in oil.

THE SERIOUS INDIVIDUAL

I say, that's not a bad idea! You don't mind if I
make a note of it?

THE OLD MAN

Go right ahead.

THE SERIOUS INDIVIDUAL (*opening a large notebook*)

Place . . . (*he writes*) Date . . . (*he writes*) Time
. . . what is the hour?

THE OLD MAN

Noon — high noon. Twelve o'clock — for you.
[*Abruptly the lighting changes.*

THE SERIOUS INDIVIDUAL (*writing*)

Twelve o'clock.
[*From the left the Lover and the Young Thing enter
together, arms twined about each other. They cross
slowly to the right.*

THE LOVER

It's fate — I know it can be nothing else. It's fate,
drawing us together from the ends of the world. The
moment I first saw you, I felt a thrill; I felt something
electric. I knew that you and I had been intended
for each other since the world began. There is
something about you — something which I can't

describe — something which I can only feel; something which tells me that you were made for me.

THE YOUNG THING (*with a friendly nod to the others*)

Has n't he got the grandest line of talk?

THE LOVER

It 's not often like that; at least, so I 've been told. Often a man spends his whole life looking for the one woman who is meant for him — spends his life searching to the ends of the earth, when she may be just around the corner — and does n't find her. How tragic that must be! How tragic! Two lives blasted! But luck — Providence — call it what you will — is on my side, and I have found — you!

THE YOUNG THING (*as he pauses ecstatically*)

Go on, cutie.

THE LOVER

To be understood: that, after all, is the greatest thing in life, and I feel that you — only you — understand me. We are kindred spirits, drawn to each other. I know it. I am sure of it. I feel that you divine my thoughts before I speak them — even before I think them; that you know what I want to say before I know it myself; that you read my mind as if it were a printed book. Am I right?

THE YOUNG THING

Betcha life, kid.

THE LOVER

Will you marry me?

THE YOUNG THING

Surest thing you know!

[*They pass out of sight at the right.*

The others have watched with different expressions.
The Old Man, as always, is gently tolerant. The Girl
does not know whether to be surprised, amused — or
pitiful. The Serious Individual, openly hostile, has
been making copious notes.

THE SERIOUS INDIVIDUAL

A disgraceful exhibition, I call it; a disgraceful
exhibition. It does n't fit in at all with my ideas.
It must not be tolerated.

THE GIRL (*gently*)

They 're not well suited to one another.

THE SERIOUS INDIVIDUAL

What has that to do with it? I am concerned with
the fundamentals.

THE OLD MAN

And what are the fundamentals?

THE SERIOUS INDIVIDUAL

I know what they are. That is sufficient. I settled
them for myself long ago. I shall make a second law.
It will go right to the bottom of things : no mincing
matters, no shilly-shallying, no temporizing with
conditions for me. For the first offense, imprisonment without hard labor; for the second, imprisonment *with* hard labor; for the third — if there
should be a third —

THE OLD MAN

Hard labor without imprisonment.

THE SERIOUS INDIVIDUAL

These matters are too serious to be discussed in jest.
(*He turns to the Girl*) Come with me.

THE GIRL

What for?

THE SERIOUS INDIVIDUAL

Evidence; I will gather evidence. I will learn all there is to know about the subject. That will occupy a few minutes. Then I will deal with it — uncompromisingly.

THE GIRL

Don't be too hard on him. A man makes mistakes.

THE SERIOUS INDIVIDUAL

I never make them.

[*They go out at the right.*

The Old Man lights his pipe; puffs it.

There enters the Poet.

THE OLD MAN

Well, what are you after? If you want to know what time it is, it's afternoon — two o'clock — for you.

[*The lighting changes abruptly.*

THE POET (*referring to his watch*)

Two o'clock: quite correct. My watch hasn't stopped again. I know the time. But that's not why I came here. I came here to think. In there there's too much hustle and bustle. This is the one place where I can get away from everything.

THE OLD MAN

And what do you want to think about?

THE POET

Beautiful things. There *are* beautiful things in the Inn, aren't there?

THE OLD MAN

I have always thought so.

THE POET

I have tried to find them. When I do find them I

shall describe them in immortal verse. (*Parenthetically*) You will pardon me for referring to my efforts so frankly? To say less would be false modesty.

THE OLD MAN

What have you written?

THE POET (*with an engaging smile*)

Nothing yet.

THE OLD MAN

Why not?

THE POET

I have failed to find a subject worthy of my pen. If there are beautiful things here, where are they?

THE OLD MAN

Would you know them if you saw them?

THE POET

I have found nothing but struggle — strife — dreams that don't come true — hopes that are never realized —

THE OLD MAN

And you found nothing beautiful there?

THE POET

I found — discontent.

THE OLD MAN

It's always that way at an Inn. Kick at the service; swear at the food; make fun of the rooms; complain about the other guests; criticize the management. An' then, when you go, recommend it to your friends — if you've got any — an' tell them how much you've enjoyed it. Tell them — tell them — you'd come back if you could.

THE POET

I'm not so sure of that.

THE OLD MAN

Spend your time finding out — nothing! Look out —
when you should be looking in! But look in once
in a while to tell your neighbors how *you* think they
ought to live their lives. Make laws, and when they
don't work, make more laws. And then, if you're
not happy yourself, if you don't find anything beautiful in the Inn, blame the rest of creation — not your
own mistakes — for it!

[*From the right enters the Young Thing, followed at
varying distances by the Lover and the Serious Individual. She is audible before she is visible.*

THE YOUNG THING

Cut it out, I tell you! Cut it out! (*She turns to the
others*) Say, if you fellows know how to do it, call
him off! Call him off, I tell you!

THE OLD MAN

What's the matter?

THE YOUNG THING

A little of him goes a long ways, that's what's the
matter. I don't mind listening to him — he's got
the gift of gab, that fellow. I don't mind holding
hands with him — I've got an affectionate dis-
position, see? But when I took him for richer or
poorer, better or worse, till death do us part, I
didn't know what I was letting myself in for. I
know now, and I'm not keen about it — not one
little bit.

THE LOVER

Sweetheart!

THE YOUNG THING

Do you know what my life's like with him? Do you want me to tell you about it? All right, here goes. Can you see him tending the furnace? Not much! He's one of them romantic guys that don't like to get his hands dirty. Can you see him walking the floor nights — about a year from now — with the baby? Not if he can make me do it! He's got to sleep, or he won't be able to think up pretty things to say to me. Can you see him drying the dishes after I wash 'em? Not on your tintype! He's one of them ornamental fellows — fine to go out walking with, but no more useful inside the house than a moth-eaten umbrella! Now, what I'm going to find myself is a young husky. He don't have to have brains if he's got the sense to do what I tell him. He don't have to look like much if he forks over his pay envelope at the end of every week And I don't care if he can't talk like a professor if he knows enough to put his arm around me and give me a good squeeze once in a while.

THE LOVER

Sweetheart!

THE YOUNG THING

"Sweetheart!" That's the trouble with him! He means it. It isn't kidding: it's the real thing. He's stuck on me — the poor nut — so he's married me, and he thinks I'm going to work for him the rest of my life! (*She turns on him*) Why couldn't you have left well enough alone? I'd have gone on being friends — nothing more than friends — see? That would have been enough — plenty! You had to spoil it all. (*She softens*) There's a girl out there who wants you. She'd like to have you. I'm going to make her a present of you. You're hers — hers on a silver platter with watercress around it. But when it comes to yours truly, you can count me out! I resign. (*She smiles: takes him by the arm*) This way, cutie.

[*She pilots him out, right.*

THE SERIOUS INDIVIDUAL (*who has not missed a word*)

Outrageous! Simply outrageous!

THE OLD MAN

Why?

THE SERIOUS INDIVIDUAL

People must get along. People must not quarrel. I object.

THE POET

So do I. Quarreling is not beautiful.

THE OLD MAN

They're a pretty poor team. They never should have hitched up together in the first place.

THE SERIOUS INDIVIDUAL

What has that to do with the welfare of the community? How, if you please, is that related to the doctrine of the highest good? The law is no respecter of persons. Scandals like this cannot — must not — continue. It's out of the question. Why, what would society come to if we closed our eyes to this?

THE OLD MAN

If they stay married, they'll lead a cat-and-dog life.

THE SERIOUS INDIVIDUAL

What of that? Many of the best people do.

THE OLD MAN

They'll be unhappy.

THE SERIOUS INDIVIDUAL

Not if I give the matter my personal attention. I
shall settle it in the simplest of all ways. I shall
make a law requiring everybody to be happy. I
shall make a law forbidding people to be unhappy.

THE POET

That sounds like a very good idea.

THE OLD MAN

Humph! Strikes me you've made a good many
laws.

THE SERIOUS INDIVIDUAL (*proudly*)

Hundreds of them!

THE OLD MAN

What's happened to them? Where are they now?

THE SERIOUS INDIVIDUAL

They have been flouted. They have been violated.
They have been ignored. But I shall remedy that.
There is nothing wrong with the Inn that cannot be
made right with a few well-phrased statutes; nothing
out of joint that cannot be put into joint by half a
dozen pages of fine print. What we need is law —
more law — and still more law. The more laws, the
more civilization; the more civilization, the more
intelligence; the more intelligence, the more laws.
A thought has occurred to me — a thought so ab-
surdly simple that I wonder why it hasn't occurred to
somebody long ago: I shall enact a new law com-
pelling everybody to obey all old laws! As simple
as that! (*He opens his notebook*) The place . . .
(*he writes*) The date . . . (*he writes*) The time . . .

THE OLD MAN

Evening.   Six o'clock — for you.

[*The lights change suddenly.*

THE SERIOUS INDIVIDUAL (*writing*)

Six o'clock.

THE OLD MAN

And you — what do you think about it?

[*He turns to the Poet.*

THE POET

I'm still waiting.

THE OLD MAN

Waiting — for what?

THE POET

For something beautiful; for something so beautiful that I may immortalize it in verse.

THE OLD MAN

An' you ain't found it yet?   In the scrap that's going on here every minute; in the fight — the fight for happiness — you can't find something you can call beautiful?

THE POET

How absurd!   I begin to think that I shall never find it.

[*There enter the Girl and the Lover.*

THE LOVER

It's fate — I know it can be nothing else.   It's fate, drawing us together from the ends of the world.   The moment I first saw you, I felt a thrill; I felt something electric.   I knew that you and I had been intended for each other since the world began.   There is something about you — something which I can't describe — something which I can only feel;

something that tells me that you were made for me.

THE GIRL (*smiling*)

One makes mistakes, my dear;- but if they are n't bad mistakes, they can be mended; and sometimes bad mistakes can be mended too. (*She turns to the Old Man*) He thinks he knows —

THE LOVER (*interrupting*)

I *know* I know.

THE GIRL (*indulgently*)

Of course you do, dear. (*She turns back to the Old Man*) But I, I have remembered. I know what it was I said to you — ages ago. I am sure. (*The Old Man smiles*) We have found each other. There is much that has come between — there is much that has come before — but it does n't matter. We found each other in the end.

THE OLD MAN

There 's something for you!
[*He nudges the Poet.*

THE POET

But that 's not beautiful! That 's a miserable, patched-up happiness! (*He turns to the Girl*) If he had come to you in the beginning, if, from the very first, you two had drifted into each other's arms, that would have been lovely. It would have been romantic. It would have been a fit theme for me to write about. But to accept him when somebody else discards him —

THE OLD MAN

That 's life.

THE POET

It's a wretched compromise.

THE OLD MAN

It's life.

THE POET

To take him when he himself isn't sure: that is un-
worthy.   There is only one thing you can do: turn
your back on him.   Anything else would be beneath
your dignity.

THE GIRL

Happiness — no matter how it comes — no matter
how late it comes — isn't beneath my dignity.

THE SERIOUS INDIVIDUAL (*appealing to the Lover*)

You must not do this thing.   You have chosen.   You
must stick to your choice.

THE LOVER

I don't want to.

THE SERIOUS INDIVIDUAL

The law commands.

THE LOVER

I made a mistake.

THE SERIOUS INDIVIDUAL

How do you know that you are not making another
now?   Wait!   Do nothing rash until I come back!
Wait!

[*He hurries off at the right.*

THE POET (*to the Girl*)

Give him up!   Renounce him!   Sacrifice yourself!
Your renunciation will be splendid!

THE GIRL

I would rather be happy than splendid.

THE POET

Refuse him! Give him to the woman who claimed him first! Send him back to her! Don't lower yourself by taking him after she rejected him! Where is your pride?

THE GIRL

I would rather be happy than proud.

THE POET

Think! Just think! Make a beautiful surrender! Be unhappy if you must; mourn what might have been the rest of your life, but I, I will write about you! In my undying lines your story will go thundering down the ages! Centuries after you are buried, people will murmur your name!

THE GIRL

What is to happen after I am gone does n't interest me greatly. The present is mine. And happiness is more important than anything else.

THE POET

To you, perhaps; but to me —

THE OLD MAN (*interrupting*)

Yes; what is it to you?

[*The Serious Individual reënters with the Young Thing.*

THE SERIOUS INDIVIDUAL

I have convinced her. I have made her see the light. I have shown her that her personal inclination must give way in the face of lofty ideals — my ideals. She is ready to do her duty.

THE OLD MAN (*gently, to the Young Thing*)

Is that so?

THE YOUNG THING (*brokenly*)

I don't want to! Oh, I don't want to! But I guess

he knows what he's talking about. I mean well, you see. I'm not bad. I don't want to do anything wrong.

THE POET

Bravo! I applaud your attitude!

THE YOUNG THING

There's lots of things I don't understand — oh, I know where I get off — and I s'pose this is one of 'em. I'm not a highbrow, I guess. But I do know I shouldn't have married him! (*She weeps*) I shouldn't have married him! He's not the man for me. I should have married somebody different — lots different. I should have had a chance to be — well, to be myself. That wasn't asking such an awful lot. That wouldn't have hurt anybody; I wouldn't have done any harm. And it's not too late now. But what am I going to do when he (*and she indicates the Serious Individual*) tells me just what's what?

THE SERIOUS INDIVIDUAL

You will know that you have done a fine thing. You will have set a worthy example. You will have an easy conscience.

THE YOUNG THING

An easy conscience? I've always had one so far. A lot of good it's going to do me from now on! But I guess you're right. (*She crosses pathetically to the Lover*) For better or worse — come on, cutie. I'll make another stab at it if you will.

THE GIRL

You would take him from me?

THE YOUNG THING

He says I got to. Honest, I don't want to.

THE GIRL

I want to keep him.

THE SERIOUS INDIVIDUAL

You can't. The law is on her side.

THE POET

You can't. It would n't be beautiful.

THE SERIOUS INDIVIDUAL

You must learn to subordinate your own wishes. You must learn — if necessary — to suffer.

THE GIRL

To suffer? To suffer? I will learn that soon enough. I have learnt something about it already. A wretched compromise — a miserable, patched-up happiness — that is all I am to have out of life. It is not much. I think what might have been. I know what can never be — and I, I suffer. Every woman has a right to her romance. I have been cheated out of mine. But I have gathered up its shreds, I have collected its particles, to build afresh in the hope that some day I may have my romance — miserable, wretched, patched-up that it is — but *my* romance to treasure in my memory.

THE LOVER (*feeling that it is incumbent upon him to say something*)

We are a pair of lovers.

THE GIRL (*looking at him sadly; shaking her head*)

A pair of lovers? No we. Say rather a woman who has found the man whom she must mother; a man who has found the woman who needs him so much that she will suffer for him; two human beings —

weak, frail, helpless — destined, perhaps, to make each other unhappy, but destined too, from the very beginning, for each other's arms.

THE SERIOUS INDIVIDUAL

Nevertheless you must learn.

THE GIRL

Learn what?

THE SERIOUS INDIVIDUAL (*it is his moment of triumph*)

You must learn that the most beautiful words in any language are these: "Thou shalt not!"

[*There is a tense pause.*

THE GIRL (*turning fiercely to the Old Man*)

And you — what do you say about it?

THE OLD MAN

I ain't been doing any saying at all. I've been thinking.

THE SERIOUS INDIVIDUAL (*loftily*)

Thinking? With what result?

THE OLD MAN

Thinking that it ain't up to me to say nothing. The time for saying things is past. It's up to me to do something.

(*Abruptly the lights change. It is dim now within the Inn. Outside a cold, blue moonlight beckons. To the Serious Individual*)

Night — night for you. Come with me! Come!

THE SERIOUS INDIVIDUAL

Where to?

THE SCIENTIST (*rushing in; taking his stand at one of the windows*)

Watch! Now watch!

THE OLD MAN

Come! You come!

[*Backwards he moves towards the threshold. As if hypnotized, the Serious Individual follows him.*

THE SCIENTIST

Now watch! Watch!

THE OLD MAN (*crossing the threshold*)

Come! Come!

THE CURTAIN FALLS

THE THIRD SCENE

Outside

There is no intermission between the second and third scenes. The curtain rises immediately.

Night. A great portal. Over it, a hanging lantern. On either side of it, lofty windows. The scene is but dimly lighted.

Discernible at one window is the Scientist; at the other the Poet.

The Old Man crosses the threshold, followed by the Serious Individual.

THE SERIOUS INDIVIDUAL (*terrified*)

Where — where have you taken me?

THE OLD MAN

Sonny, I don't know myself.. I only know that in there, you're not needed. Let them work out their lives for themselves. Let them fight for their happiness. Maybe — maybe that way it'll catch up with them.

THE SCIENTIST (*at his window*)

What do you see?

THE POET

Nothing.

THE SCIENTIST

That's what I claim! Once you cross the threshold, there is —

THE POET (*interrupting*)

Stop! Stop! I see something! I don't know what it is, but I see something!

THE SCIENTIST

Impossible!

[*He crosses to the Poet's window.*

THE SERIOUS INDIVIDUAL (*indicating the Poet*)

Why did n't you take him too?

THE OLD MAN

Because there 's hope for him. Did you hear what he just said?

At the window vacated by the Scientist, the Girl, the Young Thing, and the Lover become visible. They peer out intently.

THE OLD MAN (*turning to them; raising his arms as if in benediction*)

If it were in my power, it would be morning — morning for you!

(*The lighting outside the Inn does not change, but a beautiful, golden illumination gradually suffuses its interior, overflows through portal and windows, stretches its beams far into the outer darkness. With profound exaltation*)

Ah!

THE CURTAIN FALLS

LADY OF DREAMS

A FANTASTIC COMEDY

CHARACTERS

MARY — *had she married Jones*
MARY — *had she married Smith*
and the VOICES of
JOE JONES
MR. SMITH

LADY OF DREAMS

The scene is a very secret chamber in Mary's heart.

How describe it? Impossible. Perhaps hangings of neutral color — they need not be red! — will suggest it as effectively as will anything else. There will be no windows: in this innermost of all retreats what light there is comes from within. There will be no doors: here a chance comer may not enter. But somewhere in the small space — small as possible — marked off by the hangings, there will be a spot to sit down; a pile of cushions, perhaps, and comfortable ones, too, for here, in some of the gravest moments of her life, Mary comes to rest — and to dream — and to conjure up visions of what might have been.

It is upon Mary Jones that the curtain rises. She is thirty, let us admit. She has been married ten years — and she has had to struggle every year of the ten. Joe, her husband, is a nice fellow, but his virtues do not include a talent for making money; so if his wife is dressed in the style of twelve months ago, and not expensively dressed at that, and if her stockings are mercerized cotton, and not silk, and if, barring a narrow gold wedding ring, she wears no jewelry at all, we can understand it.

How describe her face? It is the face of any woman, if you will, after a decade of gallant fighting to keep the home a home; to make each dollar travel as far as two; to make the insufficient seem sufficient by a process of stretching that once begun will never be ended. It is the

*face of an undaunted combatant — marked, of course,
by the punishment it has suffered, but marked, too, by the
justified self-reliance that has come with the years. She
has fought many battles. If she radiates a fine confidence,
it is because she has earned the right to do so. She has
not always been victorious; but it has made her more
human, more appealing, more womanly. Hers is not an
unhappy face — far from it. She speaks:*

MARY JONES

You may come in. (*There is no answer. She speaks
again*) You may come in.

(*Through some unseen opening, Mary Smith enters.
Here, at once, is striking contrast. Mary Smith is so
emphatically* dernier cri *that styles rarely have time to
catch up with her. From head to foot she is enveloped
in a great, somber-hued cloak; but her gown, flashing
against that background like a golden chrysalis emerging
from a dusky cocoon, arrived this minute from the Rue
de la Paix. It is what the other women in her set will
be wearing next month — or the month after — and by
then Mary Smith will be wearing something else. It
is expensive — and it carries out the note of cold-blooded
extravagance so characteristic of her. Money — her
husband's money — is so plentiful that the thought of
conserving it never enters her head. She exchanges it
for the things that she wants — or thinks that she wants
— and they amuse her for an instant until something
newer catches her fancy.*

*One might expect her face to resemble that of Mary
Jones — after all, they are the same woman. But ten
years of indulgence have made Mary Smith's face a little
pursy — and more than a little dictatorial. The two*

might be taken for relatives; sisters, perhaps — not necessarily twin sisters)

Let me look at you. (*Mary Smith smiles*) So you and I are the same woman.

MARY SMITH

Yes; the same woman.

MARY JONES

You are what I would have been had I married Smith.

MARY SMITH

And you are what I would have been had I married — (*a gesture of distaste*) — Jones.

MARY JONES

A little difference between us!

MARY SMITH (*thanking her stars*)

Yes; just a little.

MARY JONES (*not in the least terrified by her magnificence looks at her from head to foot*)

Are you happy?

MARY SMITH (*with determination*)

I am happy. I am very happy. I have everything that life can give me. Of course I am happy.

MARY JONES

I am glad to know that.

MARY SMITH

I have a house on Fifth Avenue. My name is in the society columns nearly every day. The Peruvian Ambassador is coming for dinner to-night. Why shouldn't I be happy?

MARY JONES

Why not? Why not, indeed?

MARY SMITH

And you? Are you happy?

MARY JONES

You see me as I am. (*She gazes at Mary Smith*) You are looking well to-day.

MARY SMITH

1 know it.

MARY JONES

You are looking very well indeed.

MARY SMITH

I always look very well.

MARY JONES

You are looking your best.

MARY SMITH

I always look my best.

MARY JONES

Nobody would know that you are a day over twenty-five.

MARY SMITH

Don't smile too often. Give your face a rest. That's the secret.

MARY JONES

Your gown is becoming.

MARY SMITH (*carelessly*)

It will do.

[*Nevertheless she opens her cloak wide to display the gown.*

MARY JONES

It is very beautiful.

MARY SMITH

I am considered the best-dressed woman in my set.

MARY JONES

So I have read. (*She indicates the gown*) It cost a fortune, did n't it?

MARY SMITH

I 'm sure I don't know. I never bother with such things. I liked it, so I bought it. That 's all there is to it. I really have no idea what it cost. The bill will come in at the end of the month — or whenever it is that bills come. My secretary will pay it. Invaluable woman! Makes out checks so beautifully! (*She pauses*) You have n't a checking account, have you?

MARY JONES

No.

MARY SMITH

You pay as you go?

MARY JONES

You bet we do!

MARY SMITH

I suppose your husband — his name is Joe, is n't it?

MARY JONES

Yes.

MARY SMITH

Dreadful name — Joe! "Joe Jones" — it sounds like something indigestible! I suppose your husband gives you his pay envelope at the end of every week?

MARY JONES

Yes.

MARY SMITH

He does n't make a great deal, does he?

MARY JONES

No.

MARY SMITH

He is n't a director of any banks? — or railroads? — or mines? — or insurance companies?

MARY JONES

No. Not a single one.

MARY SMITH

So he does n't get any directors' fees — twenty-dollar gold pieces, you know —

MARY JONES (*interrupting*)

I *don't* know.

MARY SMITH (*calmly*)

That 's so; you would n't. It never occurred to me. But Mr. Smith gets many — hardly a day without one, and some days three and four. He gives them to me when he comes home.

MARY JONES

And what do you do with them?

MARY SMITH

Spend them, I suppose. They go. They go. They 're money, are n't they? I spend money. But what were we saying? Oh, yes! Your husband — Joe — does n't get any directors' fees?

MARY JONES

I know it sounds incredible, but he gets none at all.

MARY SMITH

You 're not mentioned in the society columns?

MARY JONES

Never — and I read them from end to end.

MARY SMITH

The Peruvian Ambassador never dines with you?

MARY JONES

Oh, no, indeed!

MARY SMITH

And are you happy?

MARY JONES (*with an inscrutable smile*)

You see me as I am.

MARY SMITH (*looking at her curiously*)

You're poor?

MARY JONES (*slowly*)

Well —

MARY SMITH

Very poor? You live in the slums?

MARY JONES (*laughing*)

"Slums" is such a relative term, isn't it? We don't consider them slums. No matter how badly off you are, there's always somebody worse off. They live in the slums — not you. It's all a matter of comparison. (*She pauses*) Has it ever occurred to you that at this very moment one of your former friends, strolling through the golden streets, looking out at the pearly gates, strumming tunes on a harp, might be thinking of the neighborhood in which you yourself live — as a slum?

MARY SMITH (*horrified*)

No; of course not!

MARY JONES

It hasn't struck you before? Well, let it sink in. (*She pauses*) Now we — Joe and I — consider the street we live in rather nice. I wouldn't say that we're satisfied with it — that we never hope to move into a better neighborhood. But we think it answers. (*Maliciously*) And our house, come to think of it, is very much like yours!

MARY SMITH (*surprised*)

What?

MARY JONES

It has a front door and a back door; and walls and ceilings and windows and floors. And I nearly forgot — it has an inside and an outside — one of each. (*She smiles*) But the resemblance, I am afraid, stops there.

MARY SMITH

How you startled me for a minute!

MARY JONES

The thought that your house was no better than mine would have been too terrible? (*Mary Smith nods*) Well, don't worry about it. The two can't be compared. Your house is what your house ought to be. Mine is quite appropriate to my humbler station. Why, my little house would feel lost in that great, rambling mansion of yours! It's *so* little! You could tuck all of it into your grand ballroom, and it would be lonely there. But I like to think it's nice — even though I know it is n't. You don't mind?

MARY SMITH

No; not at all.

MARY JONES

It's little — but that means that Joe's never far from me.

MARY SMITH

I should call that a disadvantage. I should like to get as far away from him as I could. "Joe Jones" — what a name!

MARY JONES

He's lived up to it: slow, steady, dependable, reliable.

MARY SMITH

And poor.

MARY JONES

Poor always. Born poor; grown up poor; poor to-day; and I suppose he'll die poor.

MARY SMITH

Do you love him? (*Mary Jones nods*) Very much?

MARY JONES

Very, very much. (*She pauses; glances keenly at Mary Smith*) Have you ever — ever — stopped loving him?

MARY SMITH (*drawing herself up*)

How absurd! I never cared for him.

MARY JONES

That's what you like to think. That would be, after you married the other man. It's what you ought to think. But are you sure? Are you quite sure?

MARY SMITH

I know my own mind.

MARY JONES

Do you? I wonder! Do you remember, in the summer, oh, years and years ago, how he told you of his plans —

MARY SMITH (*derisively*)

Glittering plans!

MARY JONES

They seemed so at the time.

MARY SMITH

He had them worked out to a nicety.

MARY JONES

Every detail.

MARY SMITH

Plans which did n't come true.

MARY JONES

That is life. They may yet come true. Who knows?
You won't deny they sounded very attractive when
he told you about them.

MARY SMITH

I was only a girl. I understood nothing.

MARY JONES

I 'm afraid he understood less.

MARY SMITH

It is n't fair to tax me with what happened years ago.

MARY JONES

You have never forgotten it. You can never forget
it. Listen: don't you hear his voice to this day?
Don't you hear it this minute?

JOE'S VOICE

Sweetheart!

MARY SMITH (*responding — despite herself*)

Joe!

MARY JONES

It is n't such an ugly name after all. It 's all in the
way you say it.

JOE'S VOICE

Sweetheart!

MARY JONES

Think back. Think back. It is night — night in
midsummer. You are in a canoe together — you
and Joe. You are floating over a lake — a big lake
— oh, miles and miles from side to side. The water

is still. There is hardly a ripple as the bow cuts
through it. And it is dark — very dark — but you
are not afraid, because Joe is there. (*The scene
begins to darken very slowly*) You lean forward, a
girl of twenty, drinking in the miracle of a summer
night. You smell the scent of balsam fir in the air.
A warm breeze touches your cheek gently — oh,
so gently. And you hear Joe's voice.

JOE'S VOICE

Sweetheart!

MARY SMITH (*surrendering completely*)

Joe! Dear Joe!

JOE'S VOICE

Mary, do you like me to hold your hands?

MARY SMITH

Yes, Joe.

JOE'S VOICE

So soft and warm! So little and so slender! Beautiful hands!

MARY SMITH

Do you think so?

JOE'S VOICE

The most beautiful hands in the world. Some day
— some day — we'll be sitting at our own fireside —
and I'll be holding them. Isn't that so, Mary?

MARY SMITH (*after a pause*)

Maybe, Joe.

JOE'S VOICE

Only maybe? Why not yes?

MARY SMITH (*hesitantly*)

Well, Joe —

JOE'S VOICE

Oh, I know what you're going to say. Don't say it. You don't have to say it.

MARY SMITH

All right, Joe.

[*Now the scene is quite dark.*

JOE'S VOICE

I'm not going to be like this always, Mary. They can't keep me down. I know it. I'm sure of it. There's something in me that's going to come to the top. And if I were married to you, Mary, if I were married to you, there'd be nothing that could stop me.

MARY SMITH (*tenderly — the tenderness of a great, purring kitten*)

Joe.

JOE'S VOICE

All that a man needs in life is something to make him want to get ahead, something, somebody to work for; something, somebody to love and to worship. That's what you could be — what you *would* be to me, Mary.

MARY SMITH

Joe; dear Joe!

[*From above a lovely, silvery light falls upon the scene. It discloses only the two women — and what we have seen before. Mary Smith is seated languorously — as if she were in a canoe. Mary Jones is somewhere in the shadows — motionless.*

JOE'S VOICE

Look: the moon has come through the clouds — just for us, Mary.

MARY SMITH

It sounds nice to hear you say so, Joe.

JOE'S VOICE

Just so that I can see your face, Mary — see your face while I tell you what wonderful things life has in store for us. Mary, we're young — just boy and girl. The future is before us. Nothing is impossible — nothing at all!

MARY SMITH

It's nice to talk — while we go drifting along.

JOE'S VOICE

Mary!

MARY SMITH

It's nice — drifting.

JOE'S VOICE

But I don't want to drift any more, Mary. I want to have you to work for. Ambition — I've got it — plenty of it. But I must have a target to aim at — and that's you! Mary, you can do for me what nobody else in the world can do. Mary, you will, won't you?

MARY SMITH (*dabbling her hand overboard*)

The water's warm to-night, Joe.

JOE'S VOICE

Mary, you heard me. Mary, listen: I mean every word I say.

MARY SMITH

The water's warm as toast.

JOE'S VOICE (*very earnestly*)

Mary, I'm not a dreamer. I know you think I am, but I'm not. I can hold my own along with the other fellows — I can do more than hold my own —

MARY SMITH (*interrupting*)

Joe, do you see how the trees along the shore are reflected in the water?

JOE'S VOICE (*distressed*)

Mary!

MARY JONES

Then he went on to talk of his plans —

MARY SMITH

Yes.

MARY JONES

The plans that never came true —

MARY SMITH

That might have come true —

MARY JONES

Only they did n't.

MARY SMITH

Such glittering plans! Every detail!

MARY JONES

I don't think he understood them himself.

MARY SMITH

I know I did n't understand them.

JOE'S VOICE

Mary, you were n't listening. Let me explain over again.

MARY JONES

That did n't help, did it?

MARY SMITH

Not at all.

MARY JONES

There was just one thought in your mind, one thought filling it, and crowding out everything else: marry

the man with the money!   Marry the man with the
money!

JOE'S VOICE (*distant*)

Mary!

MARY JONES

Out of your life!

JOE'S VOICE (*more distant*)

Mary!   Mary!

MARY JONES

Out of your life!   Out of your mind!   But into your
heart — forever!

[*The lighting gradually changes back to that in use at
the beginning of the play.*

MARY SMITH (*starting up*)

I'm forgetting.   To-night the Peruvian Ambassador
is coming to dinner.

MARY JONES (*a little wistfully*)

That must be nice.

MARY SMITH

It *is* nice.

MARY JONES

He'll sit at your right hand, wearing decorations
across his chest.   He has decorations, hasn't he?

MARY SMITH

Of course.   Dozens of them.

MARY JONES (*naïveté, perhaps — perhaps something
much different*)

I saw him once, you know.   He was driving down
Fifth Avenue in a parade.   I stood on the curb, and I
got a good look at him over a policeman's shoulder.

MARY SMITH

Did you?

MARY JONES

A fine looking man, with the loveliest moustache! Every inch a diplomat! You know what I mean: nobody would ever mistake him for a traveling salesman.

MARY SMITH

Well, hardly!

MARY JONES

And to-night he'll be your guest! It's almost too wonderful to be true! He'll come in. He'll shake your hand —

MARY SMITH (*interrupting good-humoredly*)

Kiss it.

MARY JONES

Of course! I saw that in the movies. He'll bow over your hand, and kiss it. That's foreign, isn't it? Then (*more naïveté — or something else*) he will Enthrall Everybody with his Brilliant Conversation while he Toys with his Food. It will be good food, too.

MARY SMITH

The best.

MARY JONES

I'll warrant you! A shame not to eat it; a wicked shame. But then Ambassadors never seem to eat, do they? They just peck at things, like canary birds. I shouldn't wonder if they got a snack between meals.

[*It is remotely possible that Mary Jones has been poking fun at Mary Smith; and it is remotely possible that Mary Smith is beginning to sense it. She changes the subject hastily.*

MARY SMITH

The Peruvian Ambassador and my husband are
very good friends. The Ambassador finds it well
to be on good terms with him. Mr. Smith has large
interests in Peru: banks — or railroads — or copper
mines — or something.

MARY JONES

You don't mean it.

MARY SMITH

Mr. Smith has large interests everywhere. Japan —
China — Europe — South America —

MARY JONES

You knew that when you first met him.

MARY SMITH

I knew that he was a man of importance.

MARY JONES

Mother found out.

MARY SMITH

Mother found out about every young man who was
attentive to me.

MARY JONES

You could hardly have called Mr. Smith a young
man — even ten years ago.

MARY SMITH

Why not? He was only fifty then.

MARY JONES

Only fifty!

MARY SMITH

In the prime of life — he said so himself.

MARY JONES

Only fifty, with no hair to speak of.

MARY SMITH

I did n't marry him for his hair.

MARY JONES

A wicked old man, with two divorced wives, and a gouty foot.

MARY SMITH (*sweetly*)

Gout is a rich man's disease. Your husband will never have gout.

MARY JONES

My husband will never have a divorced wife — let alone two.

MARY SMITH

Humph! A divorced wife is a hallmark of social standing.

MARY JONES

You would n't say that if you were the divorced wife.

MARY SMITH

Mr. Smith was unhappily married before he met me. A man makes mistakes. He had made his.

[*Very slowly the scene begins to darken.*

MARY JONES

Two of them.

MARY SMITH

But they were made, were n't they? And because they were made, I was so much the safer. It 's a dangerous thing to marry a man when he 's so young that he does n't know his own mind — he may change it some day. I did n't have to worry about that with Mr. Smith. I could rely on his maturity. I knew he had reached years of wisdom. I was marrying a man — not a boy.

SMITH'S VOICE (*cold — clear — impersonal — like an icicle*)

Exactly.   Quite so.   Exactly.

MARY SMITH

The best love is not the love that comes first, but the love that comes last.   A love like that will endure.

SMITH'S VOICE

Quite so.   Exactly.   Quite so.

[*It is now quite dark.*

MARY JONES

But he's so old!   And so bald!   And so ugly!

MARY SMITH

And so rich!   Remember, I've found out all about him.

MARY JONES

He's been divorced twice.

MARY SMITH

What of it?

MARY JONES

Once wouldn't be so bad.   But twice!

MARY SMITH

That means that other women, before you, have seen something good in him.

SMITH'S VOICE

Precisely.   Well said.   Precisely.

MARY JONES

I'm afraid!   I'm afraid!

MARY SMITH

Child, there's no reason for it.

[*A pair of searchlights, pointing well upwards, suddenly cast brilliant beams, never at rest, quivering from side to side, outwards from the scene.   Mary Jones is seated,*

her hands tensely at her sides. She is leaning forward,
trying to fathom the darkness.

MARY JONES

I 'm afraid! Oh, I 'm afraid!

SMITH'S VOICE (*cool; amused*)

Is this the first time you have ridden in an automobile?

MARY JONES

Not the first time; but I 've never gone so fast. Won't you please tell him to slow down?

SMITH'S VOICE

The car rides like silk. The road 's like velvet. There 's no danger, I assure you. He 's an excellent driver. I brought him over from France myself. He 's a thoroughly competent man. Everything I have is of the best.

MARY JONES

I don't doubt that; but I 'm frightened.

SMITH'S VOICE

Raoul, *pas si vite.* (*The beams quiver less*) Is that better?

MARY JONES

Yes; thank you.

SMITH'S VOICE

After we 're married, you 'll have a car of your own: two, if you want.

MARY JONES

I don't know if I 'll want any.

SMITH'S VOICE (*amused*)

You 'll acquire the taste soon enough. It will grow on you unawares. Money! Money! Money! The things it can buy! The comforts it can give you!

The luxuries it can pour into your lap! The unpleasantnesses from which it can save you! The annoyances, the petty vexations, the multitude of little pin pricks that it can keep far away from you! Once you've known what it's like, you'll never want to be without it — and as my wife, you will never be without it.

MARY JONES

Oh, I know that, Mr. Smith.

SMITH'S VOICE

I am a generous man. I can afford to be generous. I shall expect my wife to live up to my position — to represent me with dignity. And I shall be the last to complain if that should be expensive. I expect it to be expensive. I am prepared. You can't have something worth while unless you are willing to pay well for it; and I am willing; always willing. No matter how much you spend, I shall never ask you to retrench. I have never denied myself anything. I should not ask it of my wife.

MARY JONES (*after a pause*)

Don't you think we might turn around now?

SMITH'S VOICE

We've turned already. You didn't notice it. The car rides so beautifully that you can hardly tell what it's doing.

MARY JONES

Oh.

SMITH'S VOICE

It's not good for me to be out more than an hour at a time. We will be back in a few minutes now. Is your coat buttoned up tightly?

MARY JONES

Yes; thank you.

SMITH'S VOICE

Make sure. The night air is dangerous.

MARY JONES

Yes; I am finding it so.

SMITH'S VOICE

And what do you mean by that?

MARY JONES

I don't know. Oh, I don't know.

SMITH'S VOICE

I think I understand. You mean you are weakening.

MARY JONES

Weakening — that is the word.

SMITH'S VOICE

I don't care what the word is so long as the result is what I want it to be. Do what I want. Explain it to yourself as you please.

MARY JONES (*after a pause*)

Mr. Smith, just what do you offer me?

SMITH'S VOICE

Everything. Anything and everything.

MARY JONES

That is too much.

SMITH'S VOICE

What you don't want, you don't have to take; but what you do want is yours. (*He pauses*) Have you ever walked along the street and looked into a shop window, and wanted something — something you could n't have? As my wife, that will never happen.

MARY JONES

But isn't it happening to *you* this minute? Aren't you wanting something which you, perhaps, can't have?

SMITH'S VOICE (*in the tone in which he might say "touché"*)

Precisely. And it is that experience that I can spare you.

MARY JONES

Can you give me happiness?

SMITH'S VOICE

I can give you anything.

MARY JONES (*insistently*)

Can you give me happiness?

SMITH'S VOICE

I am happy. I can share my happiness with you.

MARY JONES

Can you? Will you?

SMITH'S VOICE

If you will let me. (*He pauses*) Well?

MARY JONES

Maybe.

SMITH'S VOICE

Maybe "yes?"

MARY JONES (*with a sudden revulsion of feeling*)

I don't love you! No! No! No! Never!
[*Abruptly the searchlights are extinguished. The original lighting returns quickly.*

MARY SMITH

What a remarkably foolish thing to do! How short-sighted! How very short-sighted! What you have thrown away for a childish whim!

MARY JONES

No! No!

MARY SMITH

Mother used to say that there are two natures in
every woman. There is the romantic half: the
half that catches at glamor, and is so often caught
by it. But there is the practical half, the half that
looks far into the future, the half that wonders what
is to come after the first flush of romance has worn
off, the half that says —

MARY JONES (*interrupting scornfully*)

Marry the man with the money!

SMITH'S VOICE

Exactly. Quite so. Exactly.

MARY SMITH

The half that urges her to be sensible —

SMITH'S VOICE (*distant*)

Precisely.

MARY SMITH

The half that examines everything calmly —

SMITH'S VOICE (*far distant*)

Well put! Well put, indeed!

MARY SMITH

The half that protects her against herself.

MARY JONES

Does she want protection? Even if she needs protection, what woman wants it? There is another
half: the half that has n't mattered to you. There
is the half that urges her to seize what is lovely in
life, to seize it because it is so fleeting; there is the
half that tells her that only her heart can lead her to

true happiness; the half that tells her to throw her life on to the gaming table as if it were worth nothing — because only in that way can it ever be worth anything!

MARY SMITH (*steadily*)
You will admit that I might have done worse.

MARY JONES (*after a pause; wistfully*)
Lady of dreams, woman that I might have been, I will admit that I might have done better!
[*She throws herself into the other woman's arms.*

MARY SMITH (*petting her*)
There! There! (*She embraces her*) There! We can't all have everything. With what we have we must be content.

MARY JONES (*raising a shining face — odd that it should shine, but it does*)
And do you imagine that I am not content? You have so many things that I have n't — so many, many — but I, I have no regrets — not a single regret!

MARY SMITH (*completely misunderstanding her*)
That 's right. Be brave.

MARY JONES
Be brave? Who needs bravery? You or I? Lady of dreams, sometimes when I am alone, sometimes when I 'm afraid that I don't appreciate how good, how very good life has been to me, I conjure up the vision of you. I will you out of nothingness: out of thin air and memories, and you come. And then I say to myself that you — the woman I might have been — have so much — and yet so little! And I

pity you!   From the bottom of my heart I pity you,
because I have so little — and it is so much!

[*Slowly Mary Smith turns her back.*

MARY JONES

People envy you, don't they?   They fawn on you.
They see you for a moment, and that's an event in a
day.   They read about you.   They think of you
as a wonderful golden butterfly, surrounded by every
luxury, cushioned by every comfort, sheltered from
the world, far, far away from anything that might
cause you even an instant's pain.   They think of
you as something too glorious to be real, and they
wish they were in your place.   But I, I look into
your heart, lady of dreams, because it might have
been my heart, and when I see how empty it is,
I thank God that I am what I am!

[*Mary Smith has not said a word.   With her back
turned, enveloped from head to foot in her great cloak,
she is motionless — as motionless as a garment hung on
the wall . . .*

A door slams loudly.

JOE'S VOICE (*happy, cheerful*)

Hello, Mary!

MARY JONES

Hello, Joe!

JOE'S VOICE

Mary, I came home early.

MARY JONES

Discharged or promoted?

JOE'S VOICE

Neither one nor t'other.   To-day's a half holi-
day — have you forgotten? — and the weather's so

lovely that I thought we'd go for a walk in the park.

MARY JONES

I'll be with you in a minute, Joe.

[*She is a vain little thing, is Mary Jones, for she opens a vanity and primps shamelessly. And in the background hangs the cloak against the wall — the cloak that envelops Mary Smith.*

JOE'S VOICE

I was reading the paper coming up in the subway — are you listening, Mary?

MARY JONES

Yes, Joe.

JOE'S VOICE

There was a paragraph about the Peruvian Ambassador going to have dinner at Mrs. Smith's. Did you see that?

MARY JONES

Yes, Joe. I read it this morning.

JOE'S VOICE

I was wondering if Smith was the man you told me about — the fellow who nearly cut me out.

MARY JONES

He didn't, Joe. He never had a chance.

[*And she dabs powder on her pretty nose viciously.*

JOE'S VOICE

But it's the same man?

MARY JONES

It's the same man, Joe.

JOE'S VOICE

Now what do you think of that? And the Peruvian Ambassador going there for dinner! Mrs. Smith must be a happy woman.

MARY JONES (*shutting the vanity with a click*)
Joe, she is n't as happy as I am.
[*She crosses the little room, nonchalantly takes the cloak and throws it over her arm — there is nothing under the cloak — nothing but the hangings.*
She smiles radiantly and goes out.

THE CURTAIN FALLS

THE LUCK-PIECE
A FANTASTIC PLAY IN ONE ACT

CHARACTERS

ALBERT
ANNIE, his mother
TOM
A SAILOR
A POLICE SURGEON
A POLICEMAN

THE LUCK-PIECE

The scene is laid in a saloon in a small American seaport; the time, the first decade of the twentieth century.

The room which is disclosed at the rise of the curtain is small, squalid, and dark. At the left is the "family entrance", a door leading into the street; below it are shaded windows. At the right, a door at the head of a rickety flight of stairs, leads into the interior of the building — probably into a bedroom. At the extreme right, in back, a third door, which is open, connects with the barroom by means of an upward flight of three steps. Through it one observes the inside of a street window, a linoleum-covered floor, a table laden — but not too liberally laden — with aged "free lunch" — and nothing more.

Chairs and a few wire-legged round tables are scattered about the place. Upon one of the tables is an open bottle; next to it, two whisky glasses. The room is dirty. Liquor has been spilt upon one of the tables, and has not been mopped up. Cigarette stubs, cigar butts, torn papers, miscellaneous refuse of every kind, are scattered about the floor. Cheap, violently colored lithographs are affixed to the walls.

It is night. No lights are burning in the room itself, but a broad, intense beam comes from the barroom, silhouetting upon its door the shadow of a bent figure, which, even as we watch, collapses into a recumbent mass.

There is a pause. Then we hear the sound of a man's voice:

ALBERT (*in the barroom*)

You will, will you? (*A pause*) I told you you'd get what was comin' to you if you didn't shut up. Now you'll believe me, won't you? (*A pause. Upon the barroom door a second shadow becomes visible: the shadow of a man standing over the lower shadow*) C'm on! Shake a leg! Beat it! Get the hell outa here! (*The standing shadow kicks the recumbent one*) Out you go! Quick! C'm on! (*A pause. Then, with somewhat less assurance*) Quit your kidding, an' get up. You needn't make out I hurt you bad. I know I didn't. It would take more than one crack to make a dent in that thick skull o' yours. (*A pause*) Get up! (*Another pause. The standing figure suddenly bends over the recumbent one*) Nils! Nils! (*The standing figure shakes the recumbent figure; raises its head — it drops inertly*) Nils! Nils! (*With a sudden note of fear*) Nils!! (*The standing figure straightens up hurriedly; disappears: returns an instant later with a carafe, and pours water*) Nils! . . . Nils! (*A long pause. Then, in a horror-stricken voice*) My Gawd, I've done him in! I've killed him! (*Slowly Albert's figure rises, slowly and fearfully backs into the room, his eyes rivetted upon the object which he has left behind. Facing the door through which he has entered, he stands panic-stricken — a lean, putty-faced, chinless weakling in the late twenties or early thirties. He is coatless. About his middle is a stained apron. The sleeves of his flannel shirt are rolled up from spidery arms*) I've killed him!

(*Panting like a hunted beast, he crosses to a table, tremblingly pours out a stiff drink, and gulps it down; stands,*

*thoroughly frightened, resting one hand on the table,
wiping the cold sweat from his forehead with the other.
The light from the next room does not waver — nor
does the shadow of the recumbent mass on the floor.
Gasping, the man turns on a sickly droplight over the
centermost table; then, moving to the stairs, unable to
remove his gaze from the barroom door, he calls)* Maw!
(A pause) Maw! Maw! *(He ascends the stairs
and raps at the door at its head)* Maw! Maw, come
down here!

[*He descends again, keeping his eyes fixed on the door.*

ANNIE *(a bleary woman of sixty, sodden, but with
shrewdness written across her features, appears on the
landing. She is not in the best of tempers)*
What do you want?

ALBERT
Maw, come here.

ANNIE *(descending the stairs painfully)*
At this time o' night, to be gettin' me out of my warm
room! It's a shame, that's what I call it; a shame.
(She is at the foot of the stairs) Well, I'm here. Now,
what do you want?
[*She is half interested, half defiant, not knowing whether
to expect a welcome or a beating.*

ALBERT *(coming to her nervously)*
Maw, listen to me — listen to me —

ANNIE
Well, I'm listenin'.

ALBERT
Maw, I've killed a man! I've killed a man!

ANNIE *(stupidly)*
Eh?

ALBERT

Don't you understand, maw? I did n't mean to do it — we was just kidding — just kidding, see? — till he called me something that got me mad — he had n't ought to have done that, maw — and then — then — I hit him with the bung-starter — I did n't mean to hit him hard — honest, I did n't mean to hit him hard — but he dropped without a whisper. Maw, he 's dead, an' I killed him.

ANNIE (*with stupid horror*)

You — you killed a man?

ALBERT (*sinking at her feet*)

I killed him — killed him dead. But I did n't mean to do it. I tell you I did n't —

ANNIE (*terror-stricken*)

You killed a man! Albert, I always knowed you 'd do that some day! You, with your temper!

ALBERT

I did n't mean to hit him so hard —

ANNIE

You killed a man! They 'll take you away from me! Albert, they 'll hang you! Hang you!

ALBERT

If they catch me.

ANNIE

I won't have it, I tell you! I won't have it! (*She seizes him fiercely*) Don't I know you did n't do it without good reason, me, your own mother? It was self-defense, Albert! Remember that: it was self-defense!

ALBERT

It won't wash, maw.

ANNIE

What do you mean?

ALBERT

If I stood right with the police, maw, maybe I could get away with it. If they did n't have nothin' on me already, maybe I 'd have a chance. But with what they know about me, I ain't got no chance at all. Maw, it 's goin' to mean just one thing, an' that 's a quick finish for me!

ANNIE

Not with me here! Not with your own mother to take care o' you! (*Suddenly*) Hush! (*There is a knocking at the street door of the barroom*) Did you lock up?

ALBERT (*nodding*)

It was past closing time.

ANNIE

But you left the lights on.

[*She goes towards the barroom door.*

ALBERT (*stopping her*)

Don't go in there! They 'd see you from the street.

A DRUNKEN VOICE FROM OUTSIDE

Al! Hey, Al! Open up there! I 'm perishin' with thirst.

ANNIE (*in a whisper*)

Don't answer him.

THE VOICE

It 's Tom, Al; Tom Satterlee. Be a good fellow, an' open up.

ANNIE

Can he see — it — from where he is?

ALBERT

No.

[*The two stand motionless.   There is a final knock.*

THE VOICE

Al, if you don't open up mighty quick, I'm goin'
round to Skelly's.   I'm a good friend o' his.   He'll
look out for me if you don't.

ALBERT (*after a pause*)

He's gone.

ANNIE

He may come around here!   (*She runs to the "family
entrance" and bolts it*)   There!   Now he'll stay where
he belongs!

ALBERT

He's gone home.

[*There is a knocking at the "family entrance."*

THE VOICE (*appealingly*)

Hey, Al: it's me! Tom! I know you hear me.
C'm on — let me in.   (*A pause. Whiningly*) Al,
I want a drink.   (*Pause*) I want it bad.   (*Pause*)
I've got the money to pay for it, Al, honest! Cash
on the nail — that's me. Pay as you go, an' don't
owe no man.   (*A long pause*) Well, you don't have
to open up if you don't want to! You ain't got the
only grogshop in the world! You hear what I'm
sayin', Al? I mean it, too, every word of it! (*A
pause*) I'm goin' away, Al. (*A pause*) I'm — hic!
— going! (*A pause*) Going! Going! (*More
faintly*) Gone.

ANNIE

He's gone.

ALBERT

What's the good? There'll be another — an'
another — an' another. We can't keep the doors
locked all the time. Sooner or later somebody's
bound to come in, an' then they'll find —

ANNIE (*interrupting*)

They'll find the body of the man you killed in self-
defense! Hold on to that, Albert! Self-defense!
Self-defense till you're blue in the face!

ALBERT

Much good that's goin' to do me! Listen, maw, ain't
I been through the mill once? Don't I know what
it's like? They put you in a little room — three or
four o' them, an' one of you — an' then they ask you
questions. "What do you know about this?"
"Nothin'." Bing! (*An eloquent gesture*) Down
you go! "What do you know about this?" "Nothin'." Bing! "What do you know about this?"
"Let up, for Gawd's sake!" Bing! Hours an'
hours an' hours of it! They hit you with their
fists; an' they hit you with rubber hose; an' they
hit you with blackjacks; an' they keep on hittin'
you. An' then, when you can't hardly get up no
more they start kickin' you — kickin' you with
their heavy boots!

ANNIE

Not if you say self-defense!

ALBERT

It don't make no difference what you say, maw —
not unless you say what they want you to say.
You're in wrong — an' they want to put you in
wronger. You ain't got no chance at all.

ANNIE (*grasping him fiercely by the shoulders*)

Be a man, Al! You ain't the first that's gotten into trouble, an' you won't be the last. Pull yourself together! Think what your father would 'ave done!

ALBERT (*slumping hopelessly into a chair*)

I ain't the man my father was. I was n't cut out for this rotten business, anyhow. I would n't be in it to-day if there was any way I could get out of it.

ANNIE (*desperately*)

If you can't get away with self-defense, there's got to be something you can get away with. I'm not goin' to have them take you away an' hang you! (*She pauses; gesticulates towards the barroom*) Who's the man you killed?

ALBERT

Nils Lindquist.

ANNIE

Who's he?

ALBERT

Sailor. Sailor on a windjammer.

ANNIE

Been here before?

ALBERT

Why, sure; everybody knows him.

ANNIE

A scrapper, ain't he? Tried to rob the till, did n't he?

ALBERT

No, maw.

ANNIE (*desperately*)

But that's the story you're goin' to tell!

ALBERT

Nobody 'ud believe it — nary a soul! Big, good-natured Nils! Why, he saved up his money like a miser. He did n't have to rob no tills. Everybody knows that. Everybody knows what he 's like.

ANNIE

You c'n say he was drunk.

ALBERT (*shaking his head*)

Nobody 's ever known him to take more than three drinks.

ANNIE

He took more than three to-night.

ALBERT

You won't get nobody to believe it. Listen, maw: Nils come in here just as I was closin' up. Feelin' good, he was. Goin' to sail for home to-morrow. Talkin' about his wife an' kids. "Gif me a scuttle o' suds," he says, "an' I drink to deir healt'. Skoal!" he says. A squarehead, you know. Big, strapping fellow.

ANNIE (*as he pauses*)

Well?

ALBERT

We stands there talkin'. "You been away from home long?" says I. "T'ree year," he says, "t'ree liflong year. Like a life time. An' you want to know why I bane goin' home? You want I should tell you secret?" He pulls on a string that 's around his neck, an' he fishes out a bag about the size of a silver dollar, an' he opens it up on the bar, an' he gets out a dinky little gold four-leaf clover. "Dat 's why," he says. "Mine woman she gif me four-leaf clover when I go 'way. Bring me good luck. Yes, sir! First voyage spar fall out of rigging. Hit me on head. If I don't have dis, I bane dead man. Second voyage I bane wash overboard by big wave. Goner for sure, I tank. Put my hand on four-leaf clover — so — (*he puts his hand to his throat*) next wave wash me back. Fourt' voyage, fall down open hatchway. Any oder fallar, he get killed. But not me! Couldn't kill me. An' now, I got money in pocket, an' I bane goin' home."

ANNIE (*as he pauses again*)

Well?

ALBERT

I couldn't help kidding. I says, "You'll get home, Nils, an' you'll find your woman has lit out with some other fellow, won't you?" Just kidding, like, I says that. An' then, I never seen a man get so mad all of a sudden. Maybe she'd done somethin' like that sometime — who knows? Maybe he was scared she was goin' to do it again. But Nils gets all red in the face, an' starts cussin', and callin' me funny squarehead names, an' first thing you know, I got mad.

ANNIE (*wringing her hands*)

Albert! Albert!

ALBERT

I don't know just what happened next. Somethin' or other he called me made me see red. An' then, there was Nils layin' on the floor, all in a heap, an' me standin' over him with the bung-starter in one hand, an' his dinky gold four-leaf clover in the other.

ANNIE (*eagerly*)

Where is it now?

ALBERT

What?

ANNIE

The four-leaf clover.

ALBERT (*shrugging his shoulders*)

I don't know.

ANNIE

Well, find it, Albert.   Find it quick!

ALBERT

What for?

ANNIE

It 'll bring you luck.   Gawd knows you need it.

ALBERT (*scoffing*)

Bring me luck? A dinky little thing like that? Why, it ain't even real gold.

ANNIE (*earnestly*)

It can't do no harm, an' it might do some good. Don't take a chance.   Where did you have it last?

ALBERT

In my hand — in there.

ANNIE

What did you do with it?

ALBERT

I don't know.

ANNIE

You must 'ave had it when you come in here. I 'll find it! (*She moves towards the door, searching anxiously.   She stops;   falls to her knees*) Albert! Albert!   Here it is!

[*She has found the four-leaf clover on the floor.*

ALBERT (*with fear*)

Take it away!

ANNIE (*coming to him*)

No! Put it in your pocket!

ALBERT

Take it away! Keep it away! It's hoodooed, ain't it? It didn't do Nils any good. It ain't goin' to help me.

ANNIE (*earnestly*)

Nils wasn't wearin' it when you hit him! He'd taken it off, hadn't he? It was in your hands, wasn't it?

ALBERT

Take it away!

ANNIE (*following him*)

If he'd been wearin' it, you couldn't 'ave killed him! It was only when he took it off that his luck changed!

ALBERT (*backed up against the wall*)

If the police find it on me, they'll know it's his.

ANNIE

They won't. An' they won't find it. That's part of the luck that goes with it! (*Eagerly she stuffs it into the pocket of his flannel shirt*) I'm puttin' it in your pocket, Albert. There! Over your heart! See you don't lose it!

[*There is a hesitant series of knocks at the "family entrance" door.*

ANNIE

Shh!

[*They are motionless. A pause. A long pause.*

ALBERT (*in a sarcastic whisper*)

If that's a sample of the luck the damn thing's bringin' me, I don't want no more of it!

ANNIE (*moves stealthily to the window; peers into the street*)

It's luck, all right.   Whoever it was, he's gone away.

[*A pause.   They gaze helplessly towards the barroom door.*

ALBERT (*sneeringly*)

Luck!   Luck!   If that's what you call luck, maybe you'll tell me what we do next.

ANNIE

Can't you run away?   Hide yourself?

ALBERT

They'd catch me like a shot.

ANNIE

You could lay low.

ALBERT

Not with every sailor in the port lookin' for me. They all knew Nils, an' they all liked him.   They'd find me inside o' twenty-four hours, an' they'd tell the police — damn them!

ANNIE

I could hide you — upstairs.

ALBERT (*nodding sarcastically*)

Sure — an' that 'ud be the first place they'll come lookin' for me.   You're full o' bright ideas, ain't you?

ANNIE (*wringing her hands desperately*)

There must be some way out!   There must be!

ALBERT (*with helpless resignation*)

There ain't.   I'm caught.   I'm in a hole.   I'm done for.   If I beat it, they'll get me.   If I stay here, they'll get me.   An' it don't matter what I say: they've got me comin' and goin'.

ANNIE

No, Albert.

ALBERT

My goose is cooked, an' that's all there's to it.   I'm
a goner for sure.

ANNIE

No, Albert; no, no!

ALBERT

Golly!   I'd 'ave been better off if he'd killed me instead of me killin' him!

ANNIE (*frantically*)

Stop!   Stop!   Albert, sence your paw died you're
the only thing I've got left in the world!   I ain't a
goin' to give you up!   You're my boy; my own little
boy that I've nursed, and brought up, and watched
over!   I don't care what you've done!   I won't let
them have you!   I won't!   I won't!

ALBERT

Fat lot you've got to say about it.

ANNIE

I'm your mother, an' it's right you should come to
me when you're in trouble.   That's what mothers
are for.   (*She holds his head against her withered
breast*)   There's other fellows that have killed their
man, an' gotten away with it!   There must be thousands of 'em!   Thousands of men that nobody sus-
pects, that come an' go, that eat an' drink an' sleep,
an' nobody stops 'em!   Thousands an' thousands
an' thousands of 'em!   If they can do it, you can
do it too!

ALBERT (*showing the four-leaf clover derisively*)

Sure!   Maybe this is goin' to help me.

ANNIE (*suddenly*)

Albert! I got an idea!

ALBERT (*not particularly impressed*)

Well, shoot it.

ANNIE

When the sailor come in — when you let him in, an'
he asked for a drink — who else was there in the
barroom?

ALBERT

Nobody. I told you that once.

ANNIE

If there had been — if there had been some drunk
there, you could 'ave said *he* did it.

ALBERT (*nodding sarcastically*)

Sure thing. That would 'ave been fine. Sure.
That would 'ave been great. Only there wasn't
no drunk there.

ANNIE

You could 'ave said Nils got into a fight with the
drunk — an' the drunk killed him before you could
stop him. Then the police would grab the drunk —
see? — an' nobody 'd lay a finger on you.

ALBERT (*scoffing*)

Just as easy! Just as easy!

ANNIE (*pursuing the current of her thoughts*)

If he was drunk — real drunk — he wouldn't know
if he 'd done it or not. He wouldn't remember.
An' the police would make him own up to it. They 'd
be knockin' *him* down — they 'd be hittin' *him* with
the rubber hose — they 'd be makin' *him* say what
they wanted him to say — not you.

ALBERT (*as before*)

Great stuff! Great! Only where's the drunk?

ANNIE (*moving mysteriously nearer*)

Albert: ain't the streets full of 'em?

ALBERT

I don't get you.

ANNIE

Wasn't there two that come knockin' on the door in the last twenty minutes?

ALBERT (*still in the dark*)

What do you mean?

ANNIE (*pointing to the "family entrance"*)

Open the door. Wait. You won't have to wait long. Somebody'll come along. Somebody that wants a drink — see? If he ain't drunk already, you don't want him. Don't let him in. But if he is drunk, you lets him in, an' you locks the door, an' you keeps 'im here. You gets him drunker. You gets him blind, stupid drunk. An' while you've got 'im here, I'll be goin' after the police! (*She pauses*) I'll go slow, so's to give you plenty o' time.

ALBERT

Golly!

ANNIE

It's goin' to be the easiest thing in the world!

ALBERT (*doubtfully*)

It's goin' to be my word against his.

ANNIE

Not if he's drunk! Not if he's as drunk as you're goin' to make 'im! Don't you see, Albert? How's he goin' to prove he's been here only ten minutes — or fifteen minutes — an' not an hour? How's he goin' to prove he did n't kill the sailor — when you 're ready to swear you seen him do it?

ALBERT (*understanding*)

Seen him do it, and pulled him off Nils. He 'd 'ave gone on soaking him if I had n't grabbed him.

ANNIE

That 's right.

ALBERT (*tentatively*)

I could n't stop the fight no sooner. The drunk hit 'im an awful crack before I seen what he was doin'.

ANNIE (*nodding happily*)

Sure.

ALBERT

But I pulled him off after he 'd hit Nils once. It was too late to help Nils then. Nils was a goner. So I grabbed the drunk, an' marched 'im in here, and kept 'im —

ANNIE

While I went for the police.

ALBERT (*grinning with satisfaction*)

Nothin' to it!

ANNIE (*testing the story gleefully*)

The drunk 'll say he don't know nothin' about it.

ALBERT

But who 'll believe 'im?

ANNIE

An' maybe he 'll be so drunk that he can't open his trap at all!

ALBERT (*nodding*)

It 'll be my fault if he ain't.

ANNIE (*poking him happily in the ribs*)

Trust you!

ALBERT (*grimly*)

Trust me!

[*He rises, moves towards the door, and lays his hand on the bolt.*

ANNIE

Wait! (*She runs to her room; returns an instant later with a shawl over her head; runs back to him*) Wait! Have you got the luck-piece?

ALBERT (*showing it*)

I 'm scared. They 'll know it 's his.

ANNIE

Has it got his name on it?

ALBERT (*after examining it carefully*)

No.

ANNIE

Well, there 's more than one gold four-leaf clover in the world, ain't there? Hold on to it! Hold on to it tight!

ALBERT (*not altogether convinced*)

Ugh! (*With a grunt, he replaces the clover in his pocket*) All ready?

[*He lays his hand on the bolt again.*

ANNIE

No. Let me open it. Then I 'll be behind the door — see? — an' I can sneak out without his seein' me. (*She takes his place at the door*) Remember: the first man in — he killed Nils!

ALBERT (*nodding grimly*)

First man in — he don't know what he 's comin' in to!

ANNIE

Now we 'll wait. I 'm openin' the door.

[*She draws the bolt and turns the knob. The door*

swings open of its own accord as a man, half drunk, half asleep, who has been leaning against it, collapses into the room.   Albert catches him as he is about to fall.

ALBERT

Tom !   Tom Satterlee !   So you did n't go away after all !

TOM (*is an aged, genial, lovable, disreputably dressed down-and-outer.   He is considerably under the influence of liquor, but he is the kind of man who becomes gentler and distinctly weepy when intoxicated.   His face shows self-indulgence — but it is not vicious. Taken all in all, there is something very appealing about the old fellow.   He speaks sleepily :*)

I was kiddin' you, Al — tha' 's all.   I knew you 'd come sooner 'r later — only I thought you was never comin'.   (*He smiles vacuously*)   I 'm dry, Al.   I 'm awfully dry.   Al, I wan' a drink.

[*Over Tom's shoulder mother and son exchange glances.*

ALBERT

Sure.   That 's what we 're here for.   Drink — all the drink you like.   (*He pilots Tom to a chair*)   Come over here and sit down.   That 's right — sit down. (*In answer to Annie's questioning look, he nods emphatically.   Annie gathers the shawl about her head, moves silently into the doorway, and indicates the bolt.   Albert understands, and nods again*)   Just a minute, Tom.   Fix you up in a minute.

ANNIE (*in a whisper*)

I 'll give you lots of time.   I won't hurry.   Get him drunker !

[*Albert nods silently.   Annie goes, shutting the door behind her.   Albert bolts it.*

TOM (*in a gentle, querulous tone*)

Why did n't you le' me in before, Al?

ALBERT (*returning to him; gruffly*)

What are you talkin' about?

TOM

You mean t' say you did n't hear me hammerin' on the door? Both doors? First one, 'n' then the other?

ALBERT

No.

TOM

I made 'nuff noise t' wake the dead. They heard me 'way down the street. They hollered at me to cut it out.

ALBERT

I did n't hear you. I was upstairs.

TOM

With the lights on down here?

[*He jerks his thumb towards the barroom.*

ALBERT (*aggressively*)

Are you callin' me a liar?

TOM (*gently*)

No, Al! I ain't doin' that. You 're my frien' — my frien' — Al.

ALBERT

That 's good.

TOM

But it was n't right t' leave me out in the street, Al, when I wanted to come in. It was mean — tha' 's what I call it — it was downright mean. It 's a cold night, an' I ain't so young as I used to be.

ALBERT (*getting bottle and glass from the near-by table*)
Was you out there long?

TOM
Hours — 'n' hours — 'n' hours. 'N ' it's nippy to-night, Al. It 's too nippy for an old man. (*His eyes shine as Al sets the bottle and glass down before him*) Ah! there 's the stuff to warm you! (*With shaking hand he pours out a glass*) Ain't you goin' to have some with me, Al?

ALBERT
Not to-night, Tom.

TOM
Ah, g'wan. Be sociable, Al. You 're my frien'.

ALBERT
Not to-night, Tom.

TOM
All right, then. Here 's how! (*He drinks and wipes his mouth with the back of his hand*) Ah! I 'm beginnin' to feel better already! That shoots through your veins jus' like — jus' like good whisky.

ALBERT (*aggressively*)
That 's what it is.

TOM
I ain't sayin' it is n't. I was jus' jokin', Al; don't you see? Jus' jokin'.

ALBERT
Well, find some other time to joke.

TOM
You c'n take a joke, Al; sure you c'n take a joke! You 're my frien'. (*He pats the bottle approvingly*) Sure this is good whisky. I know! (*He half closes his eyes*) When I was a young fellow, we used to

have wine at the table — yes, sir! — wine with every course! (*With drunken confidentiality*) I come o' good family, Al; we used to live on the fat o' the land. I know good liquor — you bet I know.

ALBERT (*looking at him curiously*)

You come o' good family? You? — you old wharf rat!

TOM (*pouring out another drink*)

My name 's Satterlee — ain't it?

ALBERT

What o' that?

TOM (*with drunken geniality*)

Not much. Only my great-gran'-daddy signed the Declaration of Inpendendence — of Indenpenden — of Inpen — oh, you know what I mean.

ALBERT (*incredulously*)

Go on!

TOM (*gravely*)

He did, he did — so help me God! William — Henry — Satterlee — with two "e's" — not a "y." A gentleman, he was.

ALBERT

Wouldn't think it to look at you.

TOM (*nodding*)

True! 's too true! William Henry — I guess he 'd turn in his grave if he could see me to-day! So would his son — my gran'-daddy — (*just the vestige of a sigh*) so would my old man. Well, here 's how! [*He drinks.*

ALBERT (*after a pause*)

Did your folks have money?

TOM

Barrels — 'n' barrels — 'n' barrels of it.

ALBERT

Did n't you get none of it?

TOM (*shaking his head*)

They think I 'm dead. They ain't seen me in forty years. They would n't care about seeing me again. (*Reflectively*) Don't know 's I 'd care, either.

ALBERT

What did you do? Run away?

TOM

Yes.

ALBERT

Why? (*As Tom does not answer*) Did you get into trouble? Did you have to beat it? (*Eagerly*) Was the police after you?

TOM (*with the last vestiges of a former dignity*)

See here, my good man, is it any of your confounded business what I did?

ALBERT (*pouring*)

Have another drink, Tom. There. It 's on the house this time. No charge. I 'm your friend, see?

TOM (*unbending*)

Mush 'bliged.

ALBERT

Now, why did you run away? Did you steal money?

TOM

Not me!

ALBERT

Did you — knife somebody?

TOM

Say, wha' do you think I am?

ALBERT

Well, then, what did you do?   Remember I 'm your
friend, Tom.

TOM (*after obvious deliberation*)

You won't tell?

ALBERT

Course I won't.

TOM

Well, I was too keen about drownin' my luck.

ALBERT (*starting violently, and clapping his hand to his
breast pocket*)

What do you mean?

TOM

If my luck was good, I 'd drink to celebrate it —
'n' if it was bad, I 'd drink to forget it — 'n' if it
was n't good nor bad, I 'd drink to improve it.   It
did n't matter what happened — I 'd drink — see?

ALBERT

What then?

TOM

I tried to cut it out.   Lord knows I tried often
enough.   (*Slowly*)   But I could n't quite make the
grade.

ALBERT

That ain't no news.   Go on.

TOM (*very slowly*)

I don't know what happened then, Al; I don't know.
I only know that one day I thought it would be bes'
for me to go 'way 'n' let the family forget me.

ALBERT

Why?

TOM (*bowing his head*)

   I had a sister — 'n' it was n't helping her any to have
   me around — see? I thought I 'd throw up the
   sponge like a — gen'leman — instead o' waitin' to
   be counted out.

ALBERT (*nodding*)

   I see.   (*He extracts the four-leaf clover from his pocket,
   and flings it on the table*)   What do you think of this?

TOM

   What?

ALBERT

   This here.
   [*He places it in the old man's hand.*

TOM (*raising his head and examining the luck-piece*)

   Four-leaf clover, eh?

ALBERT

   Yes.

TOM

   Pretty, is n't it?

ALBERT

   Yes.

TOM

   Who 's it belong to?

ALBERT (*steadily*)

   Tom, I guess it belongs to you.

TOM

   What?

ALBERT (*insistently*)

   You took it away from Nils Lindquist.

TOM (*more and more dazed*)

   What?

ALBERT

You took it away from Nils.

TOM

What would I be taking anything away from any-body for?

ALBERT

You found it hanging around Nils Lindquist's neck. He would n't let you pay for the drinks with it, so you killed him. You remember that, don't you? Then you grabbed it, an' you had it in your hand when you come out o' that room.

TOM (*passing his hand unsteadily across his eyes*)

Say that again, Al. Say it again.

[*He is very drunk, and making an effort to pull himself together.*

ALBERT

The gold four-leaf clover — you had it in your hand when you come out o' that room — after you killed Nils.

TOM (*incredulously*)

After I — after I killed Nils? Why, Nils is a good frien' o' mine!

ALBERT

Tom, don't you remember?

TOM

Not a thing.

ALBERT

Well, have another drink. Maybe that 'll help you.

TOM (*too far gone to decline*)

Yes — another drink. Tha' 's what I need. (*Albert pours the drink. Tom drinks it during the following*) Go ahead — tell me what happened.

ALBERT

Well, you walked in — you an' Nils — about an hour ago.

TOM

Me 'n' Nils?

ALBERT

Yes.

TOM

Go on.

ALBERT

You said you was dry. You said you wanted a drink.

TOM

Yes; I remember that.

ALBERT

Nils said he was dry. He said he was drier than you.

TOM (*nodding*)

Yesh; I remember that also.

ALBERT (*concealing his satisfaction*)

You stood up at the bar — you an' Nils, the two of you together — an' after he paid for one round, you paid for another.

TOM

Yesh; tha' 's right. Firs' he paid; then I paid.

ALBERT

Nils was feelin' good. He was going home to-morrow — goin' home after three years. He was sailin' for Sweden as a passenger on a ship — as a passenger, mind you — not before the mast. He was mighty proud.

TOM (*nodding*)

Yesh; he tol' me that.

ALBERT

He 'd been drinkin' a little — but you 'd been drinkin'
a lot. You come in here together, an' you had three
or four rounds — whisky, an' beer, an' then whisky
again.

TOM (*smacking his lips*)

Good stuff — none better.

ALBERT

Then it was Nils' turn to pay for a round — you 'd
paid for the last, you see — an' he said he did n't have
no more money. It was a lie.

TOM

I knew that. I knew he was lyin'.

ALBERT

He said it because he did n't want to drink no
more.

TOM

Don't you think I knew that? Why, I knew that
right off.

ALBERT

But you seen a bag hanging at his neck — a leather
bag about the size of a silver dollar — an' you says,
"Nils, let 's see what 's on the inside o' that. Might be
a gold piece — never can tell!" And Nils grins.
"It bane gold all right," he says, an' he shows you
what 's inside — this four-leaf clover. An' you
grabs it — see? — and you says "That 's good for
another round o' drinks, ain't it, Al? Set 'em up!"
An' Nils grabs it out o' your hand, an' you grabs it
back; an' then Nils gets mad — starts callin' you
names — funny, squarehead names — an' you, you
gets mad too.

TOM (*bowing his head in his hands*)

Go on, Al.

ALBERT

Nils fetches a crack at you, an' you ducks. An' then you hits Nils alongside the head — just once — but you hits him with the bung-starter, an' you lays him out cold. (*Tom, a prey to drunken emotion, does not answer*) I ain't sayin' you wasn't right — he hadn't ought to 'ave called you names like that — but he's dead, Nils is — dead as a doornail — an' you croaked 'im.

TOM (*weeping*)

Nils! Good ol' Nils! Good ol' Nils! I didn't mean to kill him!

ALBERT

It don't make no difference what you didn't mean. You done it, an' that's all there's to it.

TOM (*weeping*)

Killed him! Killed a good frien' o' mine! Killed ol' Nils! A good fellow if there ever was one! Why, I had nothin' against Nils!

ALBERT

That's the way them things happen.

TOM (*hopelessly befuddled*)

Only an hour ago he wush alive — why, I remember it ash well ash if it wush shis moment — alive, 'n' joshin' me, 'n' drinkin' wish me —

ALBERT (*highly pleased with the turn of events*)

That's right.

TOM (*echoing the story that has been told him*)

He wush tellin' me how he wush goin' back to Sweden —

ALBERT

After three years.

TOM

Yesh; goin' back ash a passenger on a boat — no more shipping before the mast for him. He wush proud o' that — don't blame him — he had a right to be proud. Goin' home, Nils wush — after three years.

ALBERT (*prompting him*)

An' then you seen the bag he had hangin' at his neck —

TOM

No.

ALBERT (*disregarding his denial*)

You says, "Might be a gold piece in it."

TOM (*emphatically*)

No!

ALBERT (*trying to convince him by raising his voice*)

An' when you finds it 's a gold four-leaf clover, you snatches it from him to pay for the drinks!

TOM (*still more emphatically*)

No! !

[*Something deep down — so deep down in the old man that even the liquor he has drunk cannot affect it — is speaking for Tom.*

ALBERT (*openly hostile*)

What d'ye mean? You admitted it a minute ago, didn't you?

TOM (*with immense — if drunken — dignity*)

I might 'ave killed him — God help me — I don't remember that. But I didn't steal his gold piece.

A great-gran'shun of William Henry Satterlee might kill — but he would n't steal!

ALBERT (*placing the clover in his hand*)

You stole this!

TOM

No!

ALBERT

I say you did!

TOM

An' I shay I did n't!

[*He seizes the luck-piece — holds it for an instant — raises it — throws it aimlessly — through the open door of the barroom — through the open door upon which the shadow of a recumbent mass is still silhouetted.*

ALBERT

You killed him!

TOM

Maybe.

ALBERT

You stole the gold piece!

TOM

Never! Never! (*The effort has been too much for his drunken equilibrium. He half collapses, half sits in a chair at the table. He raises his glass*) Good ol' William Henry! Here's how!

[*He drinks.*

In the meantime a most extraordinary thing has begun to take place in the barroom. The recumbent mass has moved. It rises slowly, painfully — resolves itself into the greatly exaggerated shadow of a man.

He is unsteady on his feet. He totters. He puts his hands to his head. He straightens up slowly. Then

*he bends and picks up something from the floor. We
see what it is for the man's shadow moves off of the
door — all but the outline of his hand, immensely
magnified, in which, for an instant, we see the gigantic
shadow of a four-leaf clover.*

*Then all shadow disappears as the man moves out
of the path of the beam, and the door becomes a blank
patch of light.*

*All of this might have been visible to Tom had he
once turned his eyes in that direction, for, with a glass
in his trembling hand, he is facing the right. Albert,
however, glaring at Tom, panting, breathless at the
thought that his victim is rejecting the story which he so
meekly accepted a few minutes ago, can have seen nothing.*

ALBERT (*leaning earnestly across the table*)

Look here, Tom, you ain't goin' back on me — goin'
back on your friend?

TOM

I didn't steal.

ALBERT

You don't remember what you done, that's the mat-
ter. Listen: you come in here with Nils, didn't you?
You had three or four drinks with Nils — that right?
He paid for one, an' you paid for the next — c'rect?
Then you gets into an argument with Nils — mean
old squarehead, stingy as they make 'em —

TOM (*interrupting*)

I didn't steal.

ALBERT (*controlling his anger*)

You wanted him to pay for another round. That
was only right, an' I'm with you, Tom. You was
right — I'll swear to that —

TOM

I did n't steal.

ALBERT

He had a gold piece around his neck. A gold piece worth a dozen rounds o' drinks —

TOM

I did n't steal. (*Unsteadily he fills his glass, once more reduced to maudlin weeping*) I thought you wush my frien', Al. I thought you wush my frien'.

ALBERT

I 'm the best friend you 've got.

TOM (*with drunken solemnity*)

You ain't, Al — you ain't. I 'm dishappointed in you. You lied to me, did n't you?

ALBERT

What do you mean?

TOM

You lied to me about one thing, Al. Maybe — maybe you lied to me about the other.

ALBERT (*snarling with rage*)

What?

TOM

I did n't steal from him. Maybe I did n't kill him. (*He sways to his feet*) Be a good fellow — tell the truth, Al. You 've been kiddin' me. Tha' 's all. What? You 've been kiddin' me! Good joke! Ha! Ha!

ALBERT (*furiously*)

If you don't believe me —

TOM

You bet I don't.

ALBERT

If you don't believe me, go into the barroom and look for yourself!

[*On the instant a shadow flashes on to the door — the shadow of a giant poising a hand above his head — and in the shadowy hand, the shadow of a huge knife, ready to strike.*

TOM (*drunk as a lord, but determined*)

I'll go. I'm not afraid. I'll go. Watch me.

[*He shuffles unsteadily towards the door — a long, difficult way, for he cannot steer himself in any one direction for two consecutive feet.*

ALBERT (*watching his zigzag progress*)

You'll find his body — Nils Lindquist's body — right where you left it — on the floor.

[*The shadow moves — is ready to kill.*

TOM

Aw' ri'. Aw' ri'. If it's there, I'll find it. You bet I'll find it. Watch me.

ALBERT (*leaping suddenly into his path*)

No, you don't!

TOM (*stopping*)

What?

ALBERT

Don't you think I see what you got in the back of your head? You want to get in that room — what? You want to let yourself out through the street door — eh? An' then you beat it? Pretty cute — only it ain't goin' to work with me.

TOM (*gently*)

I wasn't goin' to run away.

ALBERT (*confronting Tom*)

I go in first — see? — an' I puts the key in my pocket before you makes a move.

TOM (*gently insistent*)

I was n't goin' to run away.

ALBERT

You won't — I won't let you. (*Brutally he flings Tom to one side, strides across the threshold, enters the barroom. An instant's pause. Then we hear his voice*) Gawd a'mighty!

[*The shadow has disappeared. Albert's shadow is suddenly flung upon the door — and from behind another shadow leaps upon him and plunges a knife into his back. . . .*

There is never a sound from the next room. For a few seconds the two figures — slayer and slain — blend into one as their shadow sways grotesquely on the door. Then they resolve into two again as one slumps gently to the ground, and the other stands erect.

Of the happenings in the next room Tom has seen absolutely nothing. Indeed, having been thrust aside by Albert, Tom, with a philosophic shrug of his shoulders, has lurched back to the table, and has occupied himself with the difficult task of pouring yet another drink. Try as he will, he finds it next to impossible to guide the stream into the glass. To simplify matters he seats himself, with his back to the door, and by resting both elbows on the table seeks to steady his shaky hands.

Presently, without turning his head, he speaks.

TOM

Well, Al? (*As he speaks, a gigantic figure appears upon the threshold — a Swedish sailor, dressed in the habiliments of his trade, huge, broad of shoulder, deep-chested, with the characteristically light hair and engagingly frank features of his race. He is wiping off the blade of a claspknife. He seizes it, ready again for action as Tom sleepily inquires once more)* Well, Al?

[*The sailor smiles, closes up his knife, and slips it into a pocket. He moves towards Tom.*

TOM (*endeavoring now to move the glass to his lips without spilling its contents*)

What I want to know iss shis — are you kiddin' me, Al — or — ain't you? Tha' 's what I want to know.

NILS (*at the table*)

Hello, Tom.

TOM (*looking at him uncertainly*)

Gee, I thought you was Al.

NILS (*shaking his head*)

No. I bane Nils Lindquist.

TOM (*we may not know what thoughts are passing through his befuddled mind. He gazes at Nils incredulously; smiles; is again incredulous. He passes a shaking hand over his brow. Then, laboriously, he hoists himself to his feet; pinches the sailor's arm — then his own. Whatever the conclusion, he makes a wry face, seizes his glass of liquor, and succeeds in downing it at a gulp. A shining gold object, suspended at the throat of Nils' open shirt, catches Tom's attention. He fingers it with a smile*)

Then — then I did n't steal it?

NILS

My luck-piece? No, Tom.

TOM

Tha' 's good. Tha' 's very good. Tha' 's very, very, very good!

[*Holding on to Nils, he bursts into tears.*

NILS (*flinging a powerful arm about the old man's shoulders*) Come, Tom. Dis bane bad place for us. (*They move towards the street door*) Come, Tom. I take you home. (*They reach the door, Nils supporting the old man, who is weeping. The door is bolted. Nils unbolts it — opens it*) Come, old friend. I take you home — home.

[*They are gone — and the door is closed behind them. From the other door — the barroom door — comes a broad beam of light. It casts a shadow — the shadow of a recumbent mass. . . .*

There is a long pause. Then there is a rap at the street door.

ANNIE

It 's me, Albert!

[*The door is shaken. A pause. Then the door is shaken more vigorously.*

A VOICE

Open! Open in the name of the law!

[*The door opens. A policeman and a police surgeon enter.*

THE SURGEON

The door was n't locked.

[*The three, Annie and the two others, proceed into the room.*

ANNIE (*looking at the door in bewilderment*)

Funny! I knew he bolted it! I heard him bolt it when I left.

THE SURGEON (*looking about the empty room*)

Well, ma'am, where are they? You said they were here. Where are they?

ANNIE

Eh? (*She looks about stupidly. Calls*) Albert! Albert! It's your maw, Albert! (*There is no reply. She is utterly dazed — quite at a loss for an explanation — moves about vacantly, repeating the name of her son*) Albert! Albert!

THE POLICEMAN (*putting his finger to his head significantly*) Th' ould woman's been tellin' us a cock-an'-bull story, I 'm thinkin'.

THE SURGEON

We 'll have a look in the other room just to make sure. (*He strides into the barroom. We hear a gasp. Then we see his shadow kneeling over Albert's body. The surgeon rises, comes to the door, beckons to the policeman*) Tst!

[*The policeman goes into the next room.*

ANNIE (*completely bewildered, peers around in obvious distress*)

Albert! Albert!

THE SURGEON (*appears at the door a second time. He beckons to Annie*)

Tst! Come here a minute.

[*The old woman, distant the length of the room, staggers towards him. As she moves,*

THE CURTAIN FALLS VERY SLOWLY

ASHES OF ROMANCE

A FANTASTIC PLAY

CHARACTERS

A Man
A Woman
A Nurse

ASHES OF ROMANCE

A plain, severely simple, spotlessly clean room in a Western hospital. The bed, of metal enameled white, a reading table next to it, a stand with a pitcher of water and medicine bottles, and two chairs, a reclining chair, and an ordinary straight-backed chair, — these constitute the entire furniture of the room.

A door at the rear opens on a corridor. A window, plainly curtained in white, lights the room with the glow of late afternoon.

The bed is empty, but to one side, wrapped up snugly in the reclining chair, an old man sleeps peacefully. Emaciated, wasted, gaunt, this much we take in at a glance. But the face claims more attention. Unusual it is, perhaps because it is so usual, because so many faces resembling it in more than one detail greet one in the course of an hour's walk. Weak, pathetically weak, yet with a certain native shrewdness; hopelessly lacking in decision, yet with that peculiar twist to the lips which betokens stubbornness; and with it all, the high forehead and deep-sunken eyes (even though they are closed) of the dreamer. It is the face of the visionary — and the vagabond; the martyr — and his persecutor. It is the face which at some time gives promise, a promise rarely fulfilled; the face of the man who generally comes off second best in life's combats, who undertakes many things, and fails at most of them, whose character, aspirations, and feeble strivings after them may be summed up in a single epitaph: "It might have been."

There is a pause. Then a uniformed nurse opens the door, looks around, and goes out to reappear immediately with a gray-haired woman of some sixty odd years. The woman is laboring under extreme excitement.

THE NURSE (*at the door*)

You may see him.

THE WOMAN

Yes, yes.

THE NURSE (*barring her at the door*)

But you must control yourself.

THE WOMAN (*impatiently*)

Yes; of course.

THE NURSE

I warn you, you will find him changed.

THE WOMAN (*pushing her way in*)

Is he in here?

THE NURSE

Hush!

THE WOMAN

I want to see him! I must see him!

[*She turns towards the bed.*

THE NURSE

He's asleep. No, not there.

[*She points.*

THE WOMAN

Oh! (*She crosses hurriedly; comes to a halt before the sleeper. She is visibly moved; moved with such supreme emotion as a woman may feel only once or twice in a lifetime. It is with the greatest difficulty that she restrains her feelings. And she is almost sobbing as she rejoices in a whisper*) I'd have known him in a minute! Why, he hasn't changed! No!

Of course he has n't changed! A little thinner, and
his hair's gray, but I'd have known him! I'd have
known him!

THE NURSE (*sympathetically*)

It's long since you've seen him?

THE WOMAN

Long? Dear God! (*Her voice is almost hysterical*)
It's forty years! Forty live-long years!

THE NURSE

What?

THE WOMAN

The better part of a lifetime! Before you were
born!

[*She staggers; almost falls. The nurse hurries to her
with a chair; seats her in it.*

THE NURSE

Here. Sit down. (*She crosses quickly to the medicine
stand and pours a little water into a glass*) Drink
this.

THE WOMAN

No. No. I'm all right.

THE NURSE (*putting the glass to her lips*)

It's nothing but water. (*The woman drinks*) There.
No, don't get up. Sit here a minute.

[*There is a pause. The sleeping man stirs slightly.*

THE WOMAN

I feel better now. Thanks. (*With a gesture towards
the man*) He is sick? (*The nurse nods*) Very sick?
(*The nurse nods again*) And — and he told you to
send for me?

THE NURSE

He told us nothing.

THE WOMAN (*smiling sadly*)

Why not? What would it have mattered?

THE NURSE

He gave me a letter addressed to you. He asked me to mail it.

THE WOMAN

Well?

THE NURSE (*obviously embarrassed*)

He — he wouldn't give us the names of any of his relations, and we wanted to know —
[*She breaks off*.

THE WOMAN

Why did you want to know? (*The nurse does not answer. The solution suddenly flashes upon the woman*) Oh! You mean, because he is going to die?

THE NURSE (*unconvincingly*)

No, no! We don't expect anything like that.

THE WOMAN

Still?

THE NURSE

He is nearly seventy years old — and sometimes he is not quite rational . . .

THE WOMAN

Not quite rational?

THE NURSE

Refused to give us the name of a relative, or even a friend — and then handed me a letter to mail. Of course I copied the name and address.

THE WOMAN

You were right.

THE NURSE (*after a pause*)

You are one of his family? I couldn't tell.

THE WOMAN (*shakes her head*)

I might have been. He was engaged to me — forty years ago.

THE NURSE (*with sympathy*)

Oh! (*She glances at the woman's wedding ring*) But — ?

THE WOMAN (*raising her hand and indicating the ring with a pathetic smile*) This? I married. Of course I married. I couldn't wait — forty years. (*She pauses*) He wrote. He wrote every month, and towards the last still oftener. But I couldn't answer: I couldn't tell him to come to me. I didn't know where he wrote from. There was a different postmark on each letter. I didn't know where he was living — under what name — until you sent for me. [*The sleeping man stirs uneasily*.

THE NURSE

He'll wake up soon.

THE WOMAN

Leave me with him.

THE NURSE (*nods. Moves towards the door. Stops*)

You will remember that he is a very sick man —

THE WOMAN

Yes.

THE NURSE

And when he talks — (*she searches for the correct phrase*) — he is not always quite coherent.

THE WOMAN

I'll remember. Thanks.

THE NURSE

If you want me, there's a bell.

[*She indicates its location and goes. There is a long pause. The old man sleeps. A tear courses down the woman's face. She wipes it off with a handkerchief . . . The man's eyes open and close again.*

THE MAN

A little water, please. (*The woman hastens to the side and brings him a glass. He sips. She watches him intently. As he is about to raise the glass to his lips for a second time their eyes meet. He pauses; puts the glass down slowly*) You are not the regular nurse?

THE WOMAN (*in a bare whisper*)

No.

THE MAN

They have changed nurses?

THE WOMAN (*hardly audible*)

No.

THE MAN

I would n't like them to do that. Still — (*he pauses to look at her with mild curiosity*) — your face seems familiar. (*In a low voice*) Who are you?

THE WOMAN

You don't know, William?

THE MAN (*shakes his head slowly, as if the effort to remember were too much for him*)

I don't think so.

THE WOMAN

You are sure you don't know?

THE MAN (*hesitantly*)

You look — like some one I *used* to know.

THE WOMAN

Yes?

THE MAN (*as if afraid to say it*)

You look like *her*. But she — she wasn't as old as you are — (*suddenly bethinking himself, with great courtesy*) — I beg your pardon.

THE WOMAN (*smiling sadly*)

No; she wasn't as old — forty years ago.

THE MAN (*half to himself*)

She had brown hair, and her voice — her voice was so different — it was sweeter. And then her figure wasn't so full. (*He looks at her*) Her eyes were like yours. (*Courteously*) You are related to her, perhaps?

THE WOMAN (*rather bitterly*)

Related — yes.

THE MAN (*smiling happily*)

I am glad to know you, then. (*His hand finds hers; presses it; continues to hold it*) It is so long since I have seen any of her family. (*There is a long pause. Then, almost timorously*) She — she is well, I hope?

THE WOMAN

Very well, yes.

THE MAN (*reassured*)

She looked so pretty the last time I saw her; so full of life, so young, so altogether charming. There was a dimple in her cheek, and the line of her throat was beautiful. (*The feeble old woman at his side bows her gray head over his hand*) I hope — sometimes — she thinks of me.

THE WOMAN (*in a whisper*) Yes, William. Yes, William.

THE MAN (*looking at her with suddenly awakened interest*)

How are you related to her? (*She does not answer*)

A cousin? (*The woman shakes her head*) Then a
sister? (*Remembering*) But she had no sisters: she
was an only child. You — you must be her mother!

THE WOMAN (*sobbing quietly*)

Yes, yes! That girl who was so full of life, so charming forty years ago, I'm her mother!

THE MAN

Well, well, what a time has passed since we met! . . .
Why are you crying?

THE WOMAN

Because — because I'm glad to see you. Yes, that's
why, William.

THE MAN

You recognized me, did n't you? I'm —

THE WOMAN (*interrupting*)

Yes, William.

THE MAN

I have n't changed much, have I?

THE WOMAN

No, William. Not at all. (*She pauses*) Why —
why did n't you let me know where you were living?

THE MAN

I could n't let *her* know.

THE WOMAN

Why not?

THE MAN

I was afraid.

THE WOMAN (*in blank amazement*)

Afraid? Afraid of what?

THE MAN

You don't know? (*The woman shakes her head*)
You are sure you don't know?

THE WOMAN

How should I know, William?

THE MAN

But I thought it would be all over town. I thought
everybody would be talking about it.

THE WOMAN (*impatiently*)

What was it, William?

THE MAN (*looking at her keenly*)

You are her mother?

THE WOMAN

Yes.

THE MAN

And you won't breathe a word to her?

THE WOMAN

No, no, William.

THE MAN

I was afraid they would arrest me.

THE WOMAN (*thunderstruck*)

Arrest you? For what?

THE MAN

You didn't know?

THE WOMAN

No one else ever did, William.

THE MAN (*after a puzzled silence*)

He must have kept quiet about it.

THE WOMAN

In God's name, William, what was it?

THE MAN

I was taking a deposit to the bank for him —

THE WOMAN

For whom?

THE MAN

For her father. I lost it on the way. I knew what he was like. He would never believe. He would think I had stolen it.

THE WOMAN

So you left town?

THE MAN

That evening.

THE WOMAN (*shaking her head bitterly*)

William, they found the money the next morning!

THE MAN (*with little interest*)

Found it?

THE WOMAN

In the original envelope, with not a dollar missing!

THE MAN (*as if he had not heard her*)

I hoped they would find it, but I knew they never would.

THE WOMAN (*earnestly*)

Don't you understand me, William? They found it! Found it!

THE MAN (*without listening to her*)

I was afraid to return: they would arrest me. And I was afraid to let her know where I lived: they might trace the letters.

THE WOMAN

But you could have returned, William! There was no reason on earth that you should n't have!

THE MAN

I wrote to her as often as I dared. But it was n't safe to mail more than one letter from the same place. Even then I had to change my name.

THE WOMAN (*despairingly*)

William! William!

THE MAN

Of course, they might have found the money —

THE WOMAN (*interrupting*)

They *did*, William!

THE MAN

I gave up hope years ago. (*He pauses*) It was hard on me. To write to her, not knowing whether she was sick or well, whether she was happy or not, even whether she was dead or alive. (*He breaks off*) One day something — something inside of me said "Go to her; she wants you." I was afraid. Somebody might recognize me.

THE WOMAN

So you did n't go?

THE MAN

I *did* go. I walked up the street to her house. It was night. The lights were burning. I stood in the shadow, and then — then the door opened, and the old doctor came out — and I took one look at him, and — and my knees almost gave way under me. Perhaps she was sick! She might even be dying! Or dead! And then a hand pushed aside the shade at the window, and I saw her face. She had been crying, and looked so sad — and so lovely! I was ten feet away. But she could n't see me. I was in the darkness.

THE WOMAN (*after a pause*)

That must have been the night her father died.

THE MAN

All that I knew was that she was alive and well.

That was all I wanted to know.   I left town on the next train.

THE WOMAN

Without a word to her?

THE MAN

What was I to do?

THE WOMAN (*after a pause*)

Once a month your letters came.

THE MAN

Yes.

THE WOMAN

But she could n't answer.

THE MAN

No.

THE WOMAN

And she had so much to say to you! Sometimes she would write you letters — long letters, twenty and thirty pages. And when they were finished, when she had poured her soul out on to the paper, she had to tear the letters up! It felt as if she were destroying something made of flesh and blood, there was so much of herself in them!

THE MAN

I knew.

THE WOMAN

You knew?

THE MAN

I closed my eyes — and then I knew she was thinking of me.

THE WOMAN

She waited — but she could n't keep on waiting forever.

THE MAN

She didn't marry some one else? Don't tell me that!

THE WOMAN (*concealing the truth*)

No, William.

THE MAN

Couldn't keep on waiting forever? Was that what you said? What did you mean? (*The woman looks into his eyes*) Is she — ? (*The woman nods*) Dead! (*There is a pause*) Tell me, she loved me when she died?

THE WOMAN

She loved you.

THE MAN (*with infinite happiness*)

And my name was on her lips?

THE WOMAN

Your name, William.

THE MAN (*gently*)

You know, I *thought* she died — years ago.

THE WOMAN

But you kept on writing.

THE MAN

How was I to know? Of course I kept on writing.

THE WOMAN

But the courage to come back and take a risk for the sake of the girl you loved — that courage you didn't have!

THE MAN

It would have been dangerous.

THE WOMAN

And because it would have been dangerous, you didn't dare.

THE MAN

I didn't dare. . . . It wasn't only for myself: it was for her. If I had come back and found her different . . . !

THE WOMAN (*with complete understanding*)

The woman of your dreams was more real to you than the woman herself! (*She pauses, and her expression hardens*) William, the woman you loved died, you will never know how short a time ago. But the man she loved has been dead these many years, dead, and until this instant she didn't know it! (*There is a long pause. She rises with an effort*) I am going.

THE MAN

Back to her? (*The woman stares at him in bewilderment*) You will see her?

THE WOMAN (*after a pause*)

Yes, William.

THE MAN (*very gently*)

Remember me to her. Tell her that I am always thinking of her. Tell her that even though a lifetime has elapsed since we parted, her face is always before my eyes, her voice always in my ears. Tell her that when I am alone, sometimes, I feel the soft pressure of her hand in mine. And tell her that even if the world says she is dead, she is alive, no whit less beautiful, less winsome, less lovable, in the depths of my soul!

THE WOMAN (*with something of reverence*)

William!

THE MAN

Where I am, she is. I have only to close my eyes to feel her presence! Dead? She can't be dead!

While I live she can't die!   Somewheres — somehow
— she's waiting for me.   That's all I know.   The
rest I don't understand — and don't want to understand!   (*He gestures to the door*)   Go!

THE WOMAN

I don't want to leave you alone, William.

THE MAN (*with a smile*)

Alone?   I am never alone!

THE WOMAN (*bowing her head in sympathetic understanding*)

Then I leave you with her.

[*But the man is no longer paying any attention. His
dreaming eyes are fixed on the distance. And the
tremulous smile which hovers about his lips intimates
that the voice to which he now listens is other than
human. He does not move as the woman leaves, and
the door clicks shut behind her.*

THE CURTAIN FALLS GENTLY

NOCTURNE

A FANTASTIC PLAY

TO THE MEMORY OF WILLIAM SHARP

CHARACTERS

THE FIRST SPEAKER
THE SECOND SPEAKER
A YOUNG MAN

NOCTURNE

Midnight. The sound of rushing water. In the distance, the far distance, a gathering storm, accompanied by faint flashes of lightning, and the barely audible roll of thunder. But immediately overhead the heavens are sprinkled with stars.

Spanning from side to side, in the center, an old wooden bridge; but the twinkling light of the stars is so dim that the bridge is suggested rather than revealed; nothing but a dark mass, curving in a grotesque arc.

At either end of the bridge, dense woods, solemn poplars, masses of underbrush. In the central background, so that the bridge itself is faintly silhouetted against the distant picture, a line of tree tops, cut, here and there, by a patch of cloudy sky.

Under the bridge, many, many feet below it, running water. Not a bubbling brook, nor yet a leaping cataract, but a swollen, turgid stream, rushing onwards with vast power. And this, too, suggested, rather than seen. Never a sight of the swirling water; only the trembling reflection which the light of the stars, mirrored upon the changing surface of its eddies, casts upon the under side of the bridge. And always sound; never a roar, but a rush, as if the flood were conscious of its monstrous strength, and asserted it in this eternal voice: a voice never jubilant, never boastful, but impassive, harsh, insistent, ineluctable, nearly unchanging . . .

A flash of lightning, feeble, and followed, after a while, by the far distant rumble of thunder. For an instant the black mass of the bridge is outlined a little more clearly. The arched rail and its rude supports flash into sharp silhouette, but beyond it no human figure is seen: nothing but the clouds in the distance, and the jagged skyline of the trees beneath.

A pause. The sound of rushing water. The eerie play of the faint light it reflects to the bridge.

Again a wan flash of lightning, and as the scene darkens again we see that the bridge is no longer empty. Two figures are dimly discernible on it. Their clothes, whatever they may be, are dark, and indistinguishable from the background. But their faces stand out against the blackness as white pebbles on a moonlit beach.

One of these persons is a woman; a wealth of golden hair, streaming down her back, is occasionally visible. The other person speaks in the deep, sonorous voice of a powerful man.

There is a pause, while the sound of the rushing water continues.

The woman speaks first:

THE FIRST SPEAKER

The water! See the water! How beautiful it is to-night.

THE SECOND SPEAKER

Aye, beautiful.

THE FIRST SPEAKER

How calm, how mirrorlike, its surface!

THE SECOND SPEAKER

Aye, the surface; while beneath a mighty stream rushes onward.

THE FIRST SPEAKER

The wavelets sparkle in the crystalline light of the stars. Their spray is the splendor of a myriad jewels. They are crowned with the constellations of heaven. (*There is a pause*) The sound of the water! How it lisps as it slips through the swaying sedges! Its voice is the voice of a lover who sighs and whispers at the portals of his beloved; who speaks, and whose speech is such music as there never was on earth.

THE SECOND SPEAKER

Many have listened to that music.

THE FIRST SPEAKER

It is the music of a mother's voice as she lulls her child to rest. How gentle, how soothing, its plashing murmur! How restful, how tranquil, its cadenced ripple! (*There is a pause*) Its breath is the scent of the air of the mountains. Its breath is the exhalation of a garden of flowers. Its breath is sweet with the fragrance of clover.

[*There is a pause. Lightning, a little nearer.*

THE SECOND SPEAKER

Lightning! As if a hand brandished a flaming sword on the surface of the waters!

THE FIRST SPEAKER

Yet the waters are still peaceful. (*There is a pause*) See, beneath us: how the river slips by; how it seems to breathe words of endearment as it embraces the timbers of the bridge: With what a reverent hand it touches the crumbling wood: each touch a caress!

THE SECOND SPEAKER

A caress; and under it, the hand of death.

THE SECOND SPEAKER

The tender roots, torn from their bed, protest —
protest in silence.

THE FIRST SPEAKER

The water washes away from it everything that was
not pure; everything that was not clean. The
water leaves only the best of it.

THE SECOND SPEAKER

But even that it has taken and hurled to destruction!
See: it has passed us. (*He points away*) Look!

THE FIRST SPEAKER

No, no!

THE SECOND SPEAKER

Look, I say!

THE FIRST SPEAKER

No, no!

[*She buries her face in her hands.*

THE SECOND SPEAKER

Then *I* look. No longer beauty; no longer the wave
with jewels caught in its foam; no longer the glory
of the stars. But cruel, jagged stones, about which
the water leaps, shouts, dances, upon which it hurls
its captive, grinds its captive, rends its captive limb
from limb!

THE FIRST SPEAKER

No, no!

THE SECOND SPEAKER

Beyond, far beyond, unseen, but not to us, the water
feeds. The hungry water eats. And it is no longer
white: it is brown; it is muddy; it is soiled; it is
colored with the blood of its victims! It is churned

in its rock-ribbed cauldron, and it feasts! It feasts! . . . Do you remember?

THE FIRST SPEAKER

Yes, oh, yes!

THE SECOND SPEAKER

How it feasts!

THE FIRST SPEAKER (*after a pause*)

But here, how gentle, how tender is its strength! How smoothly it rushes onwards! How playfully its ripple seizes on the timbers of the bridge! How beguiling, how lover-like its clasp!

THE SECOND SPEAKER

Here the river wooes, adorned in stolen beauty, offering his love green branches and petals of sweet-smelling flowers. Here he wooes, with plashing phrases, with insidious eloquence, with fragrance ravished from the snow-bearing mountains. Here his victim listens, bowing as she yields to his seduction; first inclining, then bowing, bowing, bowing, ever deeper, ever lower. Presently she meets him. Her body is encircled in his chill embrace; her crown sullied, clotted by his kiss. So he bears her to the bridal bed. Not here, but there! There! And there the persuasive lover becomes a madman! A raging fiend! A beast that knows neither mercy nor compassion! And there, far below, on the rocks of sacrifice . . .

THE FIRST SPEAKER (*interrupting*)

Stop! Oh, stop!

THE SECOND SPEAKER

You have seen, and what you have seen, you remember. You, too, have heard the shrieks of his victims until they were drowned in his loud ringing laughter!

THE FIRST SPEAKER

Stop! Stop!

[*In the distance, the lightning flashes feebly. There is a prolonged roll of thunder.*

THE SECOND SPEAKER

The next day he wooes a new victim.

THE FIRST SPEAKER (*after a pause*)

How you hate the river!

THE SECOND SPEAKER (*with a shudder*)

Aye, that I do. I hate! I hate as I hate anything that is false; anything that mirrors the beauty of heaven in its face, and conceals the foulness of a thousand hells in its bosom.

THE FIRST SPEAKER (*with quiet emphasis*)

Yet — yet to this thing you call foul — you gave yourself.

THE SECOND SPEAKER

Gave myself? *Gave* myself? Not I!

THE FIRST SPEAKER

Then why do you stand here this night with me?

THE SECOND SPEAKER

For reasons which neither one of us may know!

THE FIRST SPEAKER

You did not give yourself?

THE SECOND SPEAKER

No! The river took me. Took me in the fullness of youth, in the prime of my forces, took me, but took me all unwilling, resisting, battling, fighting until I could fight no longer. And then the river had its will, had its will upon that poor mass of quivering

flesh that once had been my body . . . My body!
My strong, powerful body: only that morning had
I gloried in its symmetry reflected in the water!
[*He buries his face in his hands.*

THE FIRST SPEAKER (*gently; after a pause*)
That morning — was long ago?

THE SECOND SPEAKER
It may have been. (*He pauses*) How well I remember the day! How each moment of it, each
trifling act, is graven into my soul! The sun was hot
overhead. The standing grain in the meadows
rustled as the warm breeze swept through it. From
the road itself little columns of palpitating air floated
lazily upwards. Everything seemed parched and
brittle in the summer's heat. Only the river laughed
as it lapped its sedgy banks; only the river purled
onwards, cool, refreshing. And I, I was weary with
toil. I looked upon the rippling water; I stripped
off my earth-stained clothes; I stood naked on the
river bank. I quivered as the sucking mud gurgled
under my feet. And I flung my arms wide with a
sense of well-being, with the surge of life throbbing
through each fiber of my strong, clean body! I
looked upon the laughing river, and I laughed: for
the last time in life I laughed!

THE FIRST SPEAKER
That must have been far from here.

THE SECOND SPEAKER (*pointing*)
Yonder, where the river winds; where, like a silver
snake, it writhes into the distance. (*He pauses*)
I stepped into the water. I kicked, and the spray
scattered sparkling in the sunlight. I waded deeper.

The water came to my arm pits. I flung myself
into it, and swam. My weariness fell from me as my
garments had fallen off. I flung out my arms carelessly. I threw myself on my back, and breathed
deep. The water laved my sides; and the hot,
unwinking sun blazed down from overhead. From
the meadows I heard the low of cattle; from the
sedges the twitter of water-fowl. I closed my eyes.
I moved my limbs lazily. I floated, rejoicing in my
unneeded strength. And while I lay, with closed
eyes, plashing idly, the river bore me onwards; bore
me, all unsuspecting, nearer and nearer —
[*He breaks off. Lightning in the distance.*
Presently, as I lay paddling easily, moving my limbs
just enough to keep afloat, a chill current struck me:
a current sharp and frigid as the breath of death
itself. I gasped. I looked about. The river had
carried me far — far indeed. Gone — all gone were
the meadows. On either side lowered these rough,
these inhospitable banks. I turned. Manfully I
struck out. I swam. With every ounce of my
strength I swam, and the banks ceased gliding by.
For some time I remained where I was, while the
river surged downstream beneath me.

THE FIRST SPEAKER

And then?

THE SECOND SPEAKER

Not far away — it seemed only a few feet — though
it must have been more than I suspected, a venerable
oak stood sturdy on a crest, extending its arms as if
in welcome. I fixed my eyes on it. I fixed my
eyes on it. I swam! God, how I swam! Through

it all the sun beamed hot overhead, and the birds in
the sedges never ceased their twittering. The oak
seemed to come nearer — appreciably nearer, and
with new courage I swam. And then — again the
chill current, a death-dealing cold which turned my
flesh to lead while my muscles contracted numbly.
The oak on the crest became stationary. With
tiring limbs I flailed on, no longer lifting my arms
cleanly on each stroke, but gasping, splashing,
floundering like a novice. The oak began to recede.
The few yards which had separated me from it
began to multiply. Still I was not afraid! I
fought — I battled! My nerveless hands, urged on
by my undying will, clove the water. And faster,
ever faster, I was carried downstream. Then presently this bridge: the very bridge we stand on. I
saw it coming. With the trees, the sky, the water
itself reeling about me in a dizzy dance, I fixed my
eyes on this bridge. Beneath it reared a pillar —
a strong and massive pillar. I would grasp that, I
thought. I would hold fast to it. I would cling,
until, with renewed strength, I might climb out of
the flood which tossed me onwards like a bubble.
The bridge approached — approached at paralyzing
speed. My body was flung against the pillar with
a violence which drove the breath out of me. But I
seized the pillar; I clasped it tightly; I clung with
my fast ebbing strength. The river rushed on,
dashing itself into foam against the great beam to
which I held, and for an instant I triumphed!

THE FIRST SPEAKER

And then?

THE SECOND SPEAKER

The river waited. That was all: the river waited. I tried to climb. The sharp splinters tore my hands and feet. The chill spray of the water swept over me. I gained not an inch — not an inch! I tried to shout. From overhead I could hear the creak of ox-carts; the tread of passing feet. One shout and all man's resources to my aid! One shout! Only one! I opened my mouth: the foam choked me. I tried to shriek: the river's tumult mocked me. I clung to the rough-hewn wood, and beneath me, around me, leaping over me, as if in sport, the river, the hungry, patient river waited. What mattered a few minutes to the river? What mattered a few hours? Whether it was minutes or hours that I held fast I do not know. No longer did I try to climb: my muscles refused to answer my will. My thoughts began to turn to other things: to boyhood dreams; to gentle meadows; to the smell of new-mown hay; to the love of women. The spray no longer seemed so chill; the river so unfriendly . . .

[*He pauses.*

THE FIRST SPEAKER (*gently; reflectively*)

To me the river never seemed unfriendly.

THE SECOND SPEAKER

It must have been while I was thinking of these things that my clasp relaxed, that the tide bore me smiling, supremely indifferent to what it did next, from my rough haven. So it lulled me till I came below, there, into the seething cauldron where even the sky was blotted out for me under the iridescent foam. And then, at the last, I struck out again.

My arms lashed the water to a wilder frenzy, to a madder fury, not with the open hands of the swimmer this time, but with clenched fists, tightly closed on bits of wood and tufts of grass. Then the end. At the end, the river was merciful. For an instant I was flung high into the air. I fell, turning in my fall. My head split on a rock. (*He pauses*) I passed from life in the amplitude of my strength! And I, I died like a man!

[*Lightning flashes. The storm is now nearly overhead. There is a long roll of thunder.*

THE FIRST SPEAKER (*after a pause*)

What a man you must have been!

THE SECOND SPEAKER

For that reason I stand here and look down upon the water, and hate it! As one who understands its cunning and its strength, I hate it!

THE FIRST SPEAKER (*after a pause*)

I — I love it!

THE SECOND SPEAKER

Why?

THE FIRST SPEAKER

Because its strength contains now what was my poor strength. Because its cunning has known how to give me surcease of all that once made life unbearable to me.

THE SECOND SPEAKER

Then you — you died like a woman.

THE FIRST SPEAKER

A woman : I died like a woman.

THE SECOND SPEAKER

You did not struggle as did I.

THE FIRST SPEAKER

I struggled: but oh, so differently! (*She pauses*)
'Twas night, I think, when I slipped over the parapet.
The river beckoned, and I came. I hardly remember
how I hurtled downwards through the air. I struck
the water. It may have been chill; I did not think
of it. I floated; it may have been for a long time.
The river seemed kindly and gentle, ah, so gentle!
And cradled in its bosom I felt content, ah, so content!

THE SECOND SPEAKER (*as she pauses*)

But presently, when you drifted down below . . .

THE FIRST SPEAKER

I felt no pain, not I. The sharp stones may have
torn my flesh; they were welcome to it. For the
wound which I carried in my heart was far deeper
than any wound the river might inflict. My thoughts
were of my beloved, and thinking thus I closed my
eyes so gently that the river itself hardly knew I
passed. I died like a woman!

THE SECOND SPEAKER (*after a pause*)

You died of your own will.

THE FIRST SPEAKER

Yes. I used to think it would be so difficult to die.
I remember when I was a child, ill with some child's
illness — slight, they called it, but they knew it
might carry me off — how brightly the flame of life
blazed up within me, refusing to be quenched, strug-
gling to make me well again. I remember my mother
leaning over me, patting my pillow, tears in her eyes;
my gruff-voiced father, speaking disjointed words of
endearment; the doctor, young and very busy,

worried, feeling my pulse, and trying to look older than he was. Only *I* knew how tenaciously I was holding to life; *I* knew I should come through it.

THE SECOND SPEAKER

You came through it.

THE FIRST SPEAKER

Only to die here. It took me but a few minutes to give up that life that had been so carefully preserved. I wonder, was it worth it? Were all the trouble, all the thought and care that had surrounded me from birth to womanhood — wasted?

THE SECOND SPEAKER

Yes, wasted.

THE FIRST SPEAKER

What?

THE SECOND SPEAKER

Even the river teaches you that lesson. Not even a leaf falls into it of its own will. Not until high winds, the coming of autumn itself, have weakened its hold, does its time come. That tree, that but an instant ago, came thrashing down the flood, has lived its life, and gave it up at the command of a power which it could no longer resist. But it fought to the last! Just as I fought!

THE FIRST SPEAKER

I fought a greater thing than the river itself.

THE SECOND SPEAKER

And lost.

THE FIRST SPEAKER

And paid! (*She pauses*) I fought my own suspicion. First I loved him, and then I hated him, and then I loved him again. When first I met him I never knew that here was my destiny; here my end. He was different. He was refreshing. I rested my soul in him — (*breaking off suddenly, and turning to the other with the faint shadow of a smile*) — just as you rested your body in this water. I was happy; I was content. I felt myself folded in his love. I rested; I know not how long . . . And then, presently a chill current struck me — as it had struck you. And I fought against that current: unlike a woman, I fought! I gained: at least I thought I gained. The security that had once been mine seemed appreciably nearer — as it had seemed to you. And then, again that chill current . . .

[*She breaks off.*

THE SECOND SPEAKER

What you fought was only something within yourself!

THE FIRST SPEAKER (*with a wealth of expression*)

Only?

THE SECOND SPEAKER

What I fought was the power of the stream that thunders here beneath!

THE FIRST SPEAKER

Which of us fought the greater power?

THE SECOND SPEAKER

I did!

THE FIRST SPEAKER (*with a faint smile*)

So speaks a man who has not looked into the heart of a woman! (*She pauses again*) There came to me my last hope — even as it had come to you — even as you, in your dying struggles, clung to the timbers of this bridge. You clung with lacerated hands; I clung with a bleeding heart.

THE SECOND SPEAKER (*more gently*)

And then?

THE FIRST SPEAKER

My thoughts, like yours, turned to other things: to happier times; to long-lost days; to hours that had seemed like lifetimes in their bliss. Of these things I thought, and saw them as if through a haze: through a dim and misty curtain separating what was present from what was past. I thought; I smiled; and of a sudden the chill current no longer felt so chill to me; no longer so unfriendly. And through it all, for me — as for you —

[*She breaks off, choking.*

THE SECOND SPEAKER (*after a pause*)

What for you as for me?

THE FIRST SPEAKER (*with quiet emphasis*)

The river — waited. What mattered one short lifetime to the stream of life itself? What mattered one poor soul to the river of all souls? And so, the end. The river, my beloved river, was merciful — so merciful! I flowed back into it as once I had flowed out of it. And I, I died like a woman!

[*There is a long pause. Lightning flashes. There is a crash of thunder. The First Speaker buries her face in her hands.*

THE SECOND SPEAKER

You poor, poor creature! (*Again a long pause*) Still, if you had to do it again —

THE FIRST SPEAKER (*with a curiously wistful note*)

If I had to do it again!

THE SECOND SPEAKER

You would not do it.

THE FIRST SPEAKER

How do you know that?

THE SECOND SPEAKER

By looking into the heart of a man! (*He pauses.
Then, suddenly:*) Hist!
[*A young man rushes wildly on to the bridge. He is
dressed in conventional garments, light colored, so that
he is more visible against the background than the
previous speakers. He comes to the center of the bridge;
throws his arms upwards in frenzied supplication,
absolutely unconscious of the presence of the others.*

THE YOUNG MAN

Sweetheart! Sweetheart!

THE SECOND SPEAKER (*addressing the first speaker*)

Who is he?

THE FIRST SPEAKER (*terribly agitated*)

Who else should he be? (*She approaches the young
man*) John, I am here!

THE YOUNG MAN (*disregarding her absolutely*)

Sweetheart!

THE FIRST SPEAKER

John, can't you see me?

THE YOUNG MAN

Sweetheart, I can't live without you! I can't
stand it any longer!

THE FIRST SPEAKER (*wildly*)

No, No! My God, no!

THE YOUNG MAN

There never was anybody in my life but you! Just
you! I've tried getting along without you, but I
can't, dear, I can't!

THE FIRST SPEAKER (*turning desperately to the Second Speaker*)

What shall I do? Oh, what shall I do?

THE SECOND SPEAKER

What *can* you do?

THE FIRST SPEAKER

Maybe he will hear me!

THE SECOND SPEAKER

No.

THE YOUNG MAN

Dear, why did you leave me? Why did you do it?

THE FIRST SPEAKER

John, I am here! Standing next to you. Look at me! Look at me!

THE YOUNG MAN

Sweetheart, if you could only hear me!

THE FIRST SPEAKER

John, I do hear you! I do hear you!

THE YOUNG MAN

If you had only listened to me you never would have done it! There was no cause for it: I swear that to you!

THE FIRST SPEAKER

I know it, John. I know it now.

THE YOUNG MAN

I can't think of anything but you! I never loved you more than I love you this minute! I can't go on living without you!

THE FIRST SPEAKER (*fearfully agitated*)

John, you must! You must, do you hear? You are young. You have all of life before you! Its

struggles! Its dreams! Its ambitions! Don't give
it up, John! Don't give it up!

THE YOUNG MAN

I have tried to forget you, but I can't! I have tried
to think of other things, but you were everything
in life to me, and without you, life isn't worth
living!

THE FIRST SPEAKER

John, because I did a foolish thing, don't follow my
example!

THE YOUNG MAN

Sweetheart, I am coming!

THE FIRST SPEAKER (*turning desperately again to the
Second Speaker*)

Can't you do something to stop him?

THE SECOND SPEAKER

Nothing which you cannot do.

THE FIRST SPEAKER (*with sudden resolution*)

Then I — *won't* stop him!

[*She disappears in the darkness.*

THE SECOND SPEAKER (*as the First Speaker disappears*)

That, too, is beyond your power!

THE YOUNG MAN (*throwing off his coat, and leaping to
the rail of the bridge*) Sweetheart, somewhere you
must be listening to me! Sweetheart, somewhere
you must be looking down into my soul! Sweetheart, I am coming!

[*He poises his arms for the dive.*

THE FIRST SPEAKER (*suddenly appearing, a mystic
figure robed in white, under the bridge, and nearer
to us*)

John!

THE YOUNG MAN (*for the first time, appearing to hear her*)

Sweetheart!

[*His poised arms remain above his head, but his hands separate, as if in astonishment.*

THE FIRST SPEAKER

If you must come, come! My arms are outstretched in greeting! I am waiting for you! Hungering for you! Come to me, dearest! Come! Come!

[*The Young Man's eyes grow wide with horror and loathing. His open hands clench into a gesture of awful repulsion.*

THE YOUNG MAN (*almost shrieking his answer*)

No! No! No! (*He leaps from the rail; stands on the bridge again. Then, with terrible finality*)

She was n't worth it!

[*He turns; rushes off into the darkness.*

The First Speaker drops out of sight with a wail.

The Second Speaker, still on the bridge, folds his arms proudly.

A flash of lightning, and a deafening clap of thunder.

THE CURTAIN FALLS